To Melanie,

I hope you enjoy the
book

Best wishes

Stu Jacobson

A Quest for
EXCELLENCE

A Quest for
EXCELLENCE

The Incredible Story of the
Most Beautiful Store in the World

ﻋﻠﻰ

Ira Jacobson

R & J PRESS

Deal, New Jersey

Published by R&J Press
Deal, New Jersey

Publisher's Cataloging-in-Publication Data
Jacobson, Ira.

    A quest for excellence : the incredible story of the most beautiful store in the world / Ira Jacobson. – Deal, N.J. : R & J Press, 2008.

    p. ; cm.
    ISBN: 978-0-9802331-0-0

    1. Brielle Galleries. 2. Small business management. I. Title.

HD62.7.J33 2008
658.022-dc22   2007943350

Project coordination by Jenkins Group, Inc
www.BookPublishing.com

Printed in the United States of America
12 11 10 09 08 • 5 4 3 2 1

Dedication

I dedicate this book to my wonderful wife, Helene. Your love, support, wisdom, kindness and creativity have helped me immeasurably in my business and in my life. I love you dearly and thank you for always making me feel like I am the luckiest husband in the world.

Contents

Helen Boehm Foreword

When I learned that Ira Jacobson was writing this book, my first thought was that young professionals could learn so much from this man who built an internationally known retail business possibly in the worst location in existence. His Brielle Galleries became one of the finest retailers of *objets d'art* in the United States, attracting a clientele that included celebrities, politicians, musicians, business icons, and world leaders. However, Ira was unimpressed by any of that glamour and power. He treated every customer with the highest level of respect and appreciation, regardless of who they were.

When I first met Ira, it was during a visit to Brielle Galleries. This store, located in a little New Jersey shore town, was getting a great deal of attention because of its beauty. I wasn't sure that it was going to live up to its hype. Imagine my surprise when I found an oasis of charm, sophistication and taste. We began doing business with Ira almost that very day. Brielle Galleries became our top U.S. retailer, selling more Boehm porcelain than any other customer we had.

Those who had the opportunity to visit Brielle Galleries or to attend one of its lavish shows or events will find warm memories in the pages of this book. Those interested in the business lessons to be learned from Ira's vast experience will find that each story tells a tale of business creativity and innovation in a time before it was possible to reach anywhere in the world through just a few clicks on a computer mouse. I believe that anyone who reads this book will benefit from the lessons about business, integrity, and success reflected in it.

Throughout my years in business, I have had the privilege of meeting all kinds of people—Popes, Presidents, celebrities, socialites, art collectors and people who saved every penny to acquire one wonderful piece of art for a loved one. Among all of those people, Ira has remained someone special to me. He is the consummate professional, an innovative businessman, and a dear friend.

I hope you enjoy this book as much as I did.

Helen Boehm

Acknowledgments

When I sat down and thought about all of the people who should be thanked in this section, it was a humbling experience. There are so many people who shared in the success of Brielle Galleries and, without whose help, love, friendship and support, I never could have built the business into what it was.

Of course, our customers deserve thanks. Without them, we wouldn't have been able to create such an "oasis in the desert." They were loyal and supportive and many of them became my good friends over the years. To them, I give my sincere thanks.

I was fortunate to have attracted what I believe to be some of the greatest employees in all of retail. There were hundreds of wonderful people who worked for me over the years. I owe sincere gratitude to Eleanor Kuta, whose brilliant creativity always made us shine; Ray Blackman, who was a powerhouse at marketing; and Ruth Papereth, who was the driving force behind the success of our jewelry business. And I could have never done what I did without the inimitable Carolyn Langdon, whose years of talent, hard work, loyalty and unwavering support were truly extraordinary.

A very special thanks to the incredible Gwen Moran for all of her superb editorial assistance. We had a special bond from the beginning, and she has helped me take a lifetime of stories and advice and sculpt them into something cohesive and hopefully inspiring to others.

I am blessed with a wonderful and supportive family. I will always be thankful to my mother, Tillie, who knew better than I did where I would make my mark in the world. Thanks to my father, Morris, for teaching me kindness and compassion. Thank you to my sister, Nola, for giving me her half of the business when our mother passed away. Her generosity allowed me to fulfill my vision for Brielle Galleries. I am so proud of my children, Lisa and Danny, as well as my son-in-law, Richard, who are smart, successful, and fine people all around. I also have two incredible grandchildren, Julia and Ryan, who never fail to delight me and give me great hope for the future.

Of course, my deepest thanks go to my wife, Helene. As magnificent as Brielle Galleries was, it never held a candle to your beauty, both inside and out.

Ira Jacobson

CHAPTER 1

The Founding

How did an unruly boy from Lakewood, New Jersey grow up to rub elbows with well-known figures like Tony Randall and the Cousteau and Kennedy families? Or work with a former White House curator and Theo Fabergé, among others, to create a special porcelain egg in commemoration of the 200th anniversary of the White House? Or be invited to Israel to bestow a special gift of state to the President? This is a story which shows that anything is possible for those who have dreams and good ideas and who are willing to work hard enough to achieve what they want.

The story of Brielle Galleries, a business I co-founded and which I ran for more than a half-century, is one of following instincts, even when it meant breaking the rules. The truth is that I broke many of the so-called rules of retailing in the nearly six decades that I've been in the business.

By not listening to those who said I'd never succeed and by only following as much of conventional wisdom as made sense to me, I was able to build my family's store, Brielle China and Glass, from a tiny, run-down antique shop into Brielle Galleries, one of the world's top retailers of luxury goods and fine gifts, with a clientele that included celebrities, CEOs, Presidents and heads of state from around the world. Sometimes, I would stand in the store, filled with all of these incredible works of art, and shake my head in disbelief at the beauty around me.

I come from a family of entrepreneurs. My parents were part owners of National Produce, a wholesale produce company that had grown to locations throughout central New Jersey and in Miami. It was a successful business, and one with which I'd been involved since I was a child, even helping my father with bookkeeping when I was 12 years old.

My family lived in Lakewood, which was, at the time, a lavish resort town with dozens of hotels and a buzzing downtown. Its location, slightly west of the shorefront resort towns, and surrounded by pine trees, boasted a temperature of 10 degrees warmer than its surrounds, and that extra bit of red on the thermometer attracted affluent tourists, who could load up their luggage and easily travel the 90 minutes or so from Manhattan or Philadelphia by car or limousine.

At the time, frozen food wasn't even a consideration in the 70 posh hotels and resorts that dotted the small town, each creating three elaborate meals per day from fresh fruits and vegetables. Overflowing displays of ripe strawberries, melons and other seasonal fruits were expected at breakfast and lunch. Evening meals were laden with fresh vegetables. And most of this bounty came from National Produce. The business was thriving, and it was our family's plan for me to eventually move to Miami and take over my father's share of the company—but not before I received a good education.

Education was always valued by my parents, especially my mother, Tillie Jacobson. At 5-ft. 3-in. tall, she was a beauty with a savvy business sense and understanding of what people wanted. She was also a loving, and strong-willed woman who wanted her children to have the skills they needed to be successful in life. When she realized that my fourth-grade reading and math skills weren't up to par, she spent two hours a day with me, drilling me in my reading and arithmetic lessons. By the time I got to the fifth grade, I skipped to the seventh, and I was in the top five percent of my high school class, voted "Most Likely to Succeed."

While many high school seniors think about proms or graduation, mine was filled with thoughts of the war. World War II had not yet ended and I was facing the draft when I turned 18 in April. Growing up near the shore, I had always had a love of the water, so serving the Navy was appealing to me. However, because I was only 17, I needed my parents' permission in order to enlist. My mother only agreed because she thought I would be safer on the water than fighting alongside the ground troops. So, with my parents' reluctant support, I became a newly enlisted seaman. Within a few months, I was sent to Guam to begin serving my country.

The days at Naval Station Guam were long and arduous. I worked with a team of men who put submarines in dry dock to maintain and repair them. The harshness of many of the other sailors made me feel like a fish out of water. Since I was younger than most of them—and a northeasterner among men mostly from the deep south—I never quite fit in. However, my youth did work to my advantage in one way. Many of the submarine commanders took a liking to me because I was so young, and because I would listen, enthralled, as they would tell stories of covert operations in Tokyo Bay while war planes and Kamikaze pilots flew overhead. Thirteen months and 26 days after arriving in Guam, I was discharged.

While I was serving in the Pacific, I never lost my desire and determination to go to college. I had convinced my high school to award me my diploma early, citing my excellent grades and service to the school. However, getting college applications sent to Guam in 1945 wasn't an easy task. I contacted family members, who obtained the applications that they could and sent them to me. I was accepted to Columbia University, but they were unable to provide housing for me, so I had to decline. A cousin who was attending the University of California, Los Angeles, sent me an application to nearby University of Southern California, where I was accepted. I enrolled there in the fall of 1946. However, I had longed to go to the University of Michigan since attending my brother's graduation in 1940. It was a large, traditional campus, and I felt at home there. Once back in the States, I was able to obtain an application and transferred the following year. I graduated with a Bachelor's degree in business three years later.

During the time that I was away from New Jersey, the partners who owned National Produce had developed differences in how they wanted the company to continue, as partnerships sometimes do. The three families that owned the company decided to part ways. When the dissolution of the partnership was finalized early in 1950, my parents left the partnership with the Lakewood and Miami locations, along with a small parcel of land in Brielle, New Jersey, a tiny fishing village located almost equidistant from New York City and Philadelphia. The company had accepted the land to satisfy the debts of a produce stand that had previously occupied it and tried to generate revenue by renting it.

In order to further my education, I had planned to go to law school and was accepted to the University of Michigan Law School in April 1950. My enthusiasm for pursuing my law degree was tempered by the winds of war, which were in the air again. The United States was on the verge of war with Korea, and since I had served just over one year in Guam, the Navy could call on me at any time to serve again—a possibility that hung over me like a dark cloud. It was a small consolation that the credits I earned toward my degree would grant me Naval officer status. I remained in law school for one semester, but it was becoming clear to me that my parents needed my help with the business. The hours were long—easily 10 hours per day—and the work was arduous, hauling 100-lb. bags of potatoes, loading trucks full of virtually every kind of produce imaginable. I applied to New York University's Graduate School of Business and ultimately transferred there. Being closer to home would allow me to return to Lakewood each Friday to help my parents on weekends.

Relief came when we learned that I would not be called to serve again—my previous service had satisfied my obligation to the Navy. Yet, while one worry was gone, another was growing. My mother was watching, with growing unease, some changes in our town. As commercial aviation became more accessible and popular, Lakewood was losing many of its affluent vacationers. Now it was possible, if one had the means, to easily board an airplane and travel to Miami or other warm climates. That, combined with increasing wages of hotel employees meant that the hotels and restaurants that were our key clients would soon be struggling and, eventually, closing. More of them were using frozen foods as a way to cut costs. All of these changes were beginning to spell disaster for our produce business and our family's financial future.

At the same time, my mother had her eye on that small parcel of land in Brielle. It had housed a failing antique shop. And it was no wonder. The structure on the property was a small, cement building. A mere 1800 square feet, it was flat-roofed with tiny windows; no ventilation system or air conditioning. Worse, a major highway was being constructed almost directly over the top of the building, and the large overpass being built created both an eyesore and obstructed the view of the building from the south. With little, if any, foot traffic, it was just about the worst location possible for a retail shop of any kind.

Where others saw obstacles, my mother saw opportunity. She had always had fine taste and a knack for spotting trends. She decided that the tiny building would make a perfect gift shop. My father was skeptical but, over the years, had learned to trust her gut instincts, so he agreed.

At first, I didn't give much thought to the venture. It was my mother's endeavor, and although I thought that she could have chosen a better location, I was focused on my studies, while working for my father at the produce company. One day, my father told me he needed to speak with me.

"Ira, I need to speak with you about your mother's gift shop," he said. "I'd like for you to go and help her get it started."

I was surprised. Aside from carrying boxes and sweeping the floor, how could I possibly help her?

"But, Dad, I don't know a cup from a saucer," I joked. "What can I do?"

"Just help her for a couple of weeks," he said. The tone in his voice told me not to argue. I loved my father and knew that he was worried about the produce business and the family's financial future, so I agreed to his wishes.

When I arrived at the shop at 23 years old to help my mother, I was shocked by what I saw. It was full, from floor to ceiling, with furniture and boxes left by the former occupant. It took three days of back-breaking work just to empty the building, which also needed significant repair and remodeling to make it a suitable place for a gift shop.

The work was supposed to last two weeks, but took almost three months. During that time, we cleaned and painted. We worked with a master carpenter—a true craftsman—to build shelves to display the merchandise, and created a small wrapping room on the main floor. We had no money for carpeting, so I bought inexpensive linoleum tile and refinished the floor.

Now it was time to stock the place. Tillie was concerned that merchandise that was too expensive wouldn't sell, tying up precious capital on the shelves, so she focused on a range of items that would appeal to the affluent customers in the area, but which would not require the store to incur great expense. She showed me her selections in catalogs, asking me what I thought.

At first, I was indifferent. I was there to provide muscle—moving, painting, building—while I continued with school and, ultimately, return to the produce business. This irritated my mother, who wanted me to see the potential in her idea.

One day, she asked me to accompany her to New York on a buying trip to purchase stock for the store. We visited the giftware market at 225 Fifth

Avenue and the tabletop market at 41 Madison Avenue. When I walked into the first showroom, I was taken aback.

There were luminous glass vases and life-like porcelain sculptures. They were beautiful. However, I also saw that these items had been created with craftsmanship and care. These were more than just trinkets. They were beautifully made art. We arrived at the tabletop market and I saw how different settings could affect the feeling of a gathering and the look of a table.

For days, I couldn't get the beauty I had seen out of my head. Imagine working with these things all day! It was certainly more appealing than the excruciating physical demands of the produce business, where my day started at 1 a.m. and ended sometime after dinner. And with the business struggling as it was, even those unappealing hours seemed in jeopardy. Could this tiny, unassuming shop offer me a better quality of life?

After that trip, I delighted in seeing the shop come to life. The outside gave no indication of the beauty that was housed within. As the shop filled with items that were delicate, colorful and beautiful, I felt a deep sense of pride and accomplishment. It soon became clear to me that how an item was placed on a shelf made the difference in how it looked. I saw how important it was to group merchandise together and have the proper lighting to display it.

Brielle China and Glass opened for business on December 18, 1950—exactly one week before Christmas. It was the first time, but certainly not the last, that the nay-sayers would tell us that we were crazy. By that time of the year, the all-important retail holiday season, which used to begin on "Black Friday," the day after Thanksgiving, was over. Black Friday is named that because of the theory that most retailers operate at a loss until this unofficial start of the holiday shopping season, when they finally begin to operate at a profit or, "in the black." Of course, today the holiday selling season starts as early as October or even September, in some cases, but Black Friday remains one of the most popular shopping days of the season.

With such a late start, our friends and business associates told us that we'd never make it. We had already missed out on most of the volume of holiday shoppers, and were perilously close to the slow period of January and February. It was the first time we proved them wrong. My mother was thrifty and we drew very modest pay out of the business, putting in long hours and hiring only a part-time cleaning woman to help us keep the store tidy. That December, we turned a small profit, but it wasn't enough to sustain us through the slow winter season.

Ira's Business Rules

Know Your Market

If my mother would have listened to everyone who told her that this was a terrible location or that she opened too late to be successful, Brielle Galleries would have never existed. While our December 1950 opening wasn't ideal, my mother knew that Brielle had a thriving summer community, with tens of thousands of possible new customers traveling to the affluent Jersey shore towns surrounding Brielle for summer vacation. And, of course, with parties and celebrations throughout the summer, these people would need a gift shop. This would give Brielle China and Glass a second selling season to a desirable clientele. By understanding the area and looking at the big picture, she was able to see around the short-term setback of our late opening and see the big-picture opportunity of a location that had two selling seasons—even if it was located under an overpass.

After months of effort creating the shop, we were at a crossroads. I knew that my mother, whose health was failing, couldn't run the shop on her own. The hours were long and exhausting, and she had high blood pressure, circulatory problems, and diabetes. January and February sales wouldn't bring in enough money to keep the shop afloat. I knew that I wouldn't be going back to school—or to the produce business that seemed, for so long, to have been my destiny.

Something had shifted inside me during these months of working so closely with my mother. Even though it had been a short period of time, I felt an affinity for what we were trying to do—more so than I ever had with National Produce. I was beginning to handle some of the buying responsibilities and was learning about these fascinating creations—things I had never considered as more than pretty plates or knick-knacks. There was an artistry and craftsmanship about them that fascinated me. The shop had become more than just a part-time job, helping my mother. I found that I craved information about the pieces that were on the shelves. I wanted to learn about the artists whose craftsmanship and thought created art that had function as well as elegance and beauty. And the more I learned about them, the more I wanted to share that with our customers. This tiny shop was becoming my passion.

My mother believed that the shop was the only hope for the financial survival of my family. As smart as she was, I knew that she was probably right. So, what would have been unthinkable a year before came to pass after a few discussions. As a family, we decided to sell my father's share of National Produce, including the Miami location, and invest the resulting $15,000 in the gift shop. He would retain the Lakewood location, re-named Jacobson's Produce, and I would work full-time at the gift shop, following a new career path in a little gift shop near the sandy shores of Brielle, New Jersey.

Ira's Business Rules

Do What You Love

It would have been easy for me to justify leaving a tiny gift shop in order to get a law degree or M.B.A. After all, I could have simply said that I was securing my family's financial future by earning a degree that would allow me to provide for them. However, in the months that I helped my mother launch Brielle China and Glass, I realized that I truly loved what I was doing. I loved learning about these pieces and the artisans who made them. It was fascinating to me. Being on the shop floor, helping customers, and interacting with distributors—virtually everything about this business appealed to my social nature, my interests, and my sense of order.

So, when people scoff at what you want to do, saying that there are better ways to earn money or to be successful, think about this: How much is your happiness worth to you? If you're motivated and excited about the work that you do, your passion will show and you're more likely to be successful. If you have ideas and dreams, and you're willing to work hard—sometimes unbelievably hard—to make them happen, you can create great things. It was that passion, excitement and drive that allowed me to build Brielle Galleries into something that gave me happiness, success and fulfillment for decades.

What are you inspired to build?

CHAPTER 2

Making a Bad Location Work

The interior of Brielle China and Glass looked like a little jewel box. Custom-made fixtures of deep, burnished walnut were individually lit and showcased each object in glittering style. From the beginning, people were impressed by the inside of the shop.

Unfortunately, that was about the only good thing that anyone could say about our location. It was an unremarkable cement building. The state had seized the south side of our property to build the bridge that was being constructed over our store. It completely blocked the view from the south side. To the north, there was a traffic light, which stopped cars before they were able to really see our building. Not that there was much to see. Our building was so plain that it hardly gave a hint of what was inside. One of our customers referred to us as "an oasis in the desert"—a paragon of good taste in an area that didn't have a provider of beautiful and tasteful gifts.

On top of all of that, the flat structure had no air conditioning or ventilation, so we had to keep the doors and windows open in the warmer months. That made everything dusty and dirty, so we were constantly cleaning—dusting the shelves, sweeping the floor, wiping down countertops and walls. I had never had to swab decks in the Navy, but I sure did spend my share of time mopping the floors at our gift shop. However, the upscale clientele we were targeting wouldn't return to a place that had dust-caked merchandise and dirty giftware.

Still, as poor as the location was, there were dozens of 40 to 70-foot yachts docked in the waterways to our north and south; a sign of the wealth that resided and vacationed in the area around the shop. A renowned tourist destination, the central New Jersey shore attracted wealthy people from northern New Jersey, New York and Philadelphia who flocked there during their summers and, increasingly were building year-round homes in the area. I knew that we would be successful if we could attract and retain them as loyal customers.

However, because we owned the building outright, we had little over-head—just the taxes and what we needed to draw for living expenses. For my work, I was paid the princely sum of $25 per week—that would roughly equate to $204 in 2006. The money was paid out of the reserves that we had from the sale of National Produce. Most weeks during the summer, I worked seven days and five evenings at the shop. Other times of the year, I generally worked seven days a week and Friday nights.

As I watched the customers come and go, I began to get a true sense of what they liked—and what they didn't. My modern tastes ran counter to their traditional style. I saw what was selling and it all began to make sense. I spent time studying my customers like some people spend time studying mathematical equations or great literature. Soon, themes and patterns emerge and it all begins to make sense.

After making it through that first December, we had sold through more than one-third of our inventory and had the proceeds from the National Produce sale. Aside from the pittance we took to cover our expenses, we bootstrapped—re-investing every penny back into the business. We took the money that we had and, the next year, we decided to invest in an expansion, carpet and heating and cooling system. Our first step was to more than double the size of the shop from 1800 square feet to 4100 square feet.

This was the first of what would end up being 18 internal and external expansions over the life of the store.

People thought I was crazy for tearing apart the store so many times, but I was always thinking of ways to make it bigger and better. It's a philosophy in retail that you should move your inventory to keep it fresh, but you should avoid construction or anything that will have a potentially negative impact on the traffic flow or look of the store. But my customers loved it. We re-invented the store every time we expanded, creating fresh new mixes of inventory and introducing new products. It was part of what made people come back—to see what we would do next.

One benefit of my father being a successful and well-liked business-man was that he had a great number of contacts. He was able to find a colleague who worked at carpeting wholesaler L. Jones, a New York City company that gave us a very reasonable price on new carpet. That allowed us to afford the same posh floor covering of much more established shops on our small budget. My father was also able to help us find a heating, cooling and ventilation provider who gave us an excellent deal on new

Ira's Business Rules

Who You Know

By developing a good reputation for being honest and reliable in his produce business, my father developed a wide network of contacts who were only too happy to help out here and there when we were getting started.

Don't be afraid to tap your contacts. If you've developed relationships with colleagues over the years, you'll find that, often, they're all too eager to help you when you need it. Just be sure to return the favor when you have the opportunity.

systems for the shop. His advice was that we invest in a unit that was too large for our shop. He pointed to the future and told us that if we continued to expand, we would be left with an insufficient system and would have to make the expenditure all over again. So, we took a leap of faith and spent more than we had planned on the systems, which ended up lasting us more than 20 years.

Our inventory primarily consisted of reasonably priced table settings, giftware and glasses. I knew that to truly capitalize on this market, we needed to begin carrying upscale china and crystal to serve the bridal market. These were the days when families, especially the wealthy families at the shore, entertained in grand style. I knew that our customers would just as easily purchase a $500 crystal vase as they would a $5 picture frame—perhaps more easily so. This was an audience concerned with style, taste and quality.

When we talked about taking on the more expensive lines, my mother got nervous. I wanted to begin stocking Boehm porcelain, an exclusive line of porcelain sculptures that were made in Trenton, New Jersey. They ranged in price from $150 to more than $20,000. I believed that the line would be a perfect and unique attraction for the shop. Her answer was always the same, "We'll consider it after the bills are paid."

In retailing, as in most businesses, there's always another invoice—another place for the money to go. So, the bills were never really all paid. By the time that I was able to persuade her that the money we would have to invest in inventory would be worth it, we were too late. Another shop had taken on the line and the area was protected. We would not be able to carry it.

I was constantly confronting the remnants of my mother's and father's past. They had lost a significant amount of money and real estate holdings during the Depression, and weren't about to risk this shop by tying up much-needed capital in expensive inventory. Tillie was perfectly happy watching the shop turn a small profit, but I knew I wanted more than that. It was just a matter of figuring out how.

Ira's Business Rules

Make Sure Your Partners are on the Same Page

My parents were in their 50s when we launched the store. Their priorities were preserving their assets and incurring little risk. I was a young man who was just starting out—I was willing to take calculated risks in order to get ahead and grow the store aggressively. While we were able to work out our differences, if we hadn't had such strong family ties, that could have been very different.

It's important to have a good understanding of your partner's goals when you go into business together. Be sure that you have similar visions for growth and similar tolerance for risk. Teaming up with someone who wants to grow your business slowly while you want to make it as big as you can as quickly as you can could be a recipe for disaster. So, consider your business partner as you would a spouse—you're going to have to live with this person's personality and priorities for a long time. And getting "divorced" from a business partner can, in some cases, be messier and more difficult than getting divorced from a spouse.

CHAPTER 3

Setting a Standard

The next year, 1951, was our first full year in business, and after the first expansion we grossed $30,000 in sales. But I still had the gnawing feeling that we needed an upscale line of china to begin to capitalize on our market.

Contrary to what other retailers often do, I made it a point to not visit other specialty gift shops—or any gift shops at all, for that matter. I wanted to be sure that we were following our vision for the store and not influenced by what other retailers were doing. That doesn't mean that I didn't keep on top of the competition in other ways. I read trade magazines and talked to my suppliers, who shared ideas and information. However, I think that visiting established merchants in better locations, with larger client bases, might have seemed a bit intimidating at the time. In the beginning, I didn't want to be discouraged by them. Later, I found that we were getting along fine with our own creativity and ingenuity and didn't have the need to visit them. So, I never did.

One thing I did know from casual visits to department stores was that many retailers displayed all of their china together in one large area. I knew that we would have to truly showcase the china in order to sell it. At first, we built special window showcases that were visible from the street to attempt to attract customers. Instead of the "wall of china" that people saw when they walked into a department store—a morass of place settings in stands, all competing with each other for attention—I wanted to highlight each product individually. I worked with our carpenter to design special boxed shelving units to house each of the patterns, along with longer units to show the various accessory pieces, such as sugar bowls, creamers and covered dishes. This required stocking more than 150 patterns. I realized that most wouldn't sell well, if at all. However, giving the customer a full selection so that she or he could feel as if all of the options had been considered would make us able to sell as many as 15 percent of the patterns very well. Isolating each pattern, lighting each individually, made it a focal point, allowing customers to carefully consider them one by one.

This was a revolutionary concept at the time—devoting precious floor space to a particular brand, housed in its own room and dividing the patterns in such a way. But it worked. Customers could carefully consider each pattern without the distraction of peering around one place setting to see another.

I discussed this unique method of displaying our product when I approached Lenox about carrying their line. Lenox was the must-have china at the time, and I was determined to add it in the store. I called on their Trenton headquarters and told them about our store. However, at the time there was another retailer with locations in South Orange and Bay Head, New Jersey that was carrying Lenox. In those days, manufacturers protected their territories. If a retailer carried a line and was doing well with it, the manufacturer would not sell the line to other retailers in the area who could be deemed competitors. So, the salesperson at Lenox politely declined my request.

I made it a point to visit Lenox every few months to discuss carrying their line. I got to know the people there, but to no avail. The only New Jersey competitor I had already carried the line and it was one of the few times I dealt with territory protection. There wasn't much I could do.

18

Without Lenox, I needed to find another high-end china line to attract the bridal market. I searched and found Rosenthal, a line of fine china from Germany. While the thought of investing in this inventory made Tillie nervous, she was also beginning to see that our customers didn't have another store nearby from which they could purchase porcelain and crystal, so she agreed that we would take on the line.

Carrying Rosenthal allowed us to attract more of the bridal market in the area, as it was a time when virtually every affluent young bride received a full set of china, crystal and silver for her wedding. Soon, we added lines of crystal and sterling silver flatware so that we could meet the needs of these customers.

Of course, new product additions weren't always big hits. We added other accessories, including a beautiful line of modern lamps that I had spotted at the giftware market at 225 Fifth Avenue in Manhattan. They were housed on an entire wall of one of the galleries, and I thought that they were truly stunning. So, we were puzzled when sales of the lamps fell flat. No matter how we tried to sell them, it took us nearly four years to liquidate that inventory.

That's when I learned that you need to be sure you're buying what your customer wants and not what you, personally, prefer. That can be difficult, especially when you're in a showroom full of beautiful things that you love. But I learned to always take time to view the products through my customers' eyes. What would they think of this? Would they buy it? I pictured the homes of customers whom I had visited. How would the product look with their décor? The style at the time was mostly Colonial and traditional. If the products wouldn't go in a home that reflected those tastes, I learned that they probably wouldn't sell in my shop.

From the beginning, we knew it was critical to set a standard of impeccable taste as part of the business identity. A large steel column was surrounded by a fireplace on two sides, turning it from an eyesore into a focal point. Every detail of the shop was polished and perfected.

In merchandising, we also took chances. In addition to the investments we made in our customized fixtures, we brought in tables and set them with our crystal and china. It required us to keep more inventory on the floor, but this was a strategic move. Tillie wanted to try to develop a home decorating section, and she soon began lining up clients, so we began stocking more home accessories. That opened New York City's

Ira's Business Rules

What Does Your Customer Want?

Sometimes, it takes time to figure out the buying patterns and preferences of your customers. Although I had been studying them intently, I allowed my personal affinity for the lamps to cloud my judgment. Although they were beautiful, they weren't in sync with the more traditional and Colonial tastes of our primary customer base.

If the product doesn't move and the space isn't yielding money after a reasonable amount of time, you need to cut your losses and move on. I liquidated the lamps at a deep discount, moving them out so that I could put something else in that space—something that would produce revenue for the space it occupied.

It was an expensive lesson to learn, and we eventually had to liquidate the lamps for cost. But, after that, I always asked myself, "Is this what my customers want?" instead of "Do I like this?"

Part of the entrepreneurial experience is making mistakes. The key is to learn from them, because they often have valuable lessons. No matter how much you love a product or service, don't waste space or dollars on something that your customers aren't buying.

Decoration & Design Building to us—and a whole new world of product. There, we found antique chandeliers and unique home décor items that our customers loved.

By showing exactly how to combine the various pieces, a table setting could literally sell itself. Our tables were showpieces and we changed them frequently. I called it romancing my product. I taught my customers how to coordinate china, crystal and silver—things that they loved, but didn't know how to use together. I taught them that it's best to choose either the china or the silver that you love, that you have to have, then work from that point. If you have an ornate silver pattern, we would find beautiful plain china with a simple gold border. A heavily decorated china might go best with a thin-stemmed stemware without decoration.

Sadly, throughout this time, my mother's health was failing. The circulatory problems in her legs were making it difficult for her to spend long days in the store, so more and more of the responsibility fell on my shoulders. We built a cozy bedroom and shower in the back area of the warehouse so that she could go and rest during the day.

I was doing all of the buying for the store, and again wanted to expand into more lines of china. Her response was always the same, "You can do that after the bills are paid, Ira." But in the end, I knew that she would trust me to select what I thought was right. I had been doing all of the buying since that first trip to the New York City markets, which she arranged deliberately. She had known that I would fall in love with the products and I did.

Brielle China and Glass was beginning to come into its own. While we couldn't afford to keep everything in stock at first, we eventually were able to expand our inventory through our own growth and by negotiating better terms with vendors. We had two showrooms in addition to the main floor, and stocked a very large collection of fine tableware and crystal, with enough inventory to allow any bride-to-be to take home an entire service for a dozen or more in one of our top 12 patterns. For other patterns, she could take home at least one place setting. This expansive inventory enabled us to give our customers an unparalleled level of fulfillment. When they wanted it, we had it in stock.

While it didn't have the physical demands of the produce business, the store took up most of my time, leaving me little time for socializing. If I wasn't working in the store, I was handling the bookkeeping or reading about new products. It was all-consuming. However, a rare and fortunate exception happened in 1954. A friend and I had decided to go out on the town. We went to the nightclub at the New Irvington Hotel in Lakewood. There, I met a beautiful young woman named Helene Motiuk. She was visiting her friend's grandmother, and I was instantly taken with her. We started dating and were married two years later.

Over the years, Helene would prove instrumental in helping me with the business. She had a creative mind and put up with my long hours. For the first 10 years of our marriage, she agreed to live on the same low salary

Ira's Business Rules

Surround Yourself with People Who Believe in You

Starting your own business is challenging under the best circumstances. When you are also fighting the negativity of people in your personal life, it can only make the prospect more difficult.

Seek out people who believe in you and your mission. It's important to have the buy-in of family and friends. If my wife, Helene, hadn't been as supportive as she has been for all these years, it would have been very difficult for me to run and grow the business. By finding people who believed in me and what I was trying to do, I was able to rely on their support and encouragement during the tough times.

so that we could re-invest profits back into the business. Later, she had the idea to launch a special orders division and spearheaded that, which became an important revenue center for us. I'm sure I wouldn't have built the business to the level that it reached without her ideas and her support.

Each year, the shop grew a little. We were profitable from the beginning and our frugality, plus the proceeds of the sale of the Miami location of National Produce, allowed us to bootstrap our way through modest expansions and inventory upgrades. Rosenthal was doing well for us. A year after we landed Rosenthal, a young Lenox salesman visited my store and saw what we were doing. Impressed with what he saw, we finally landed the most important china line. After that, it was much easier to attract other high-end brands like Minton and Royal Doulton, whose management and marketing teams were reassured that Lenox had given us their vote of confidence. I expanded the galleries, which were proving to be a hit with customers and manufacturers alike.

About four years into the business, it was time to expand again. I redesigned the shop to enhance the experience of our customers, putting in a long couch for one spouse to sit while the other shopped. A small fish pond in the front of the store added a soothing touch, while providing entertainment for children, who loved to watch the fish while making wishes and tossing coins into the water.

The growth was comparatively slow and our revenue was hardly enough to sustain two families. I didn't want to live on a pittance my whole life. Helene and I married in 1956, and we wanted to start a family. I had bigger dreams for myself than just running a small gift shop.

However, when I told all of this to my mother, she wasn't concerned. She was of a different mindset and happy with how the shop was doing. As she aged, she just wanted stability and a small financial return on her time to provide for my father and her. She assumed that I would be happy with the same small investment, which would grow modestly after she and my father passed away. The thought of incurring debt was frightening to her, but in order to complete the expansion that I had in mind, we would need an infusion of capital.

I had no credit of my own at that time, so I was at the mercy of my parents to help me achieve that vision. They wouldn't hear of it. Close to the time where they were thinking about retiring, they wanted to be careful about taking on any new expenses.

This went on for several years. The shop continued to grow, but was barely making enough to support both families. I began to think that the only way I would be able to get ahead was to change my career path. I re-applied to the University of Michigan Law School. If I couldn't make it as a gift shop owner, I would go back to school for my law degree. I was accepted, and broke the news to my mother. My leaving to go back to school meant that the store would have to be sold.

It wasn't that Tillie didn't understand my ambition. She had been the one to foster it all of these years. Still, she had come to love this little shop in the nearly dozen years since we'd opened it. And, with her health failing, she knew that my departure meant that she would have to sell the store.

She agreed to do so, but then didn't lift a finger to find a buyer. She continued to come into the shop every day as though nothing had changed. When I finally sat her down and explained again that I was concerned about my future, she was thoughtful. She agreed to help me secure the $50,000 that I would need to complete the expansion. And I, in turn, notified the University of Michigan that I would not be attending law school that year.

CHAPTER 4

An Ending . . .
and a Beginning

lthough we had "bootstrapped" the business for nearly 14 years and through several expansions, it was soon clear that it was going to take more than just reinvesting our moderate profits to grow the business. We would need an infusion of cash to do two things: It would help us increase our inventory with more high-end items and to fund another expansion that would help us overcome the limitations of our location.

That loan was the risk of my life, but allowed us to expand the first story of the building from 4,100 to 8,200 square feet. We also built second and third floors on the back of the building, giving us a third-floor warehouse, office space, and additional room for galleries. We put in a tube system to move money off of the main floor, and a dumbwaiter moved product from the first floor to the second floor for wrapping.

The additions changed the dynamics of the building entirely. I was able to build new rooms devoted to house Steuben, Buccellati silver, Lalique, Baccarat, Waterford, and our prized porcelain art collections, including Cybis and Boehm. The new, larger space and our unparalleled inventory were starting to attract the attention of major competitors who came to visit our galleries. However, they couldn't duplicate our unique approach to marketing these beautiful pieces.

We continually added product and regularly changed the fixtures. Since they were all beautiful, custom-made shelves and displays, we moved them up to the third floor to our warehouse, replacing some of the commercial shelving units that were up there.

We also offered an area of discounted and lower-priced merchandise on that floor. I promoted it by placing a large sign near the cashier counter that touted the clearance merchandise. My staff disliked it—they thought it wasn't appropriate for our high-end shop—but it worked. All of the research I had done had told me that getting people to our third floor would be one of our biggest challenges. But our warehouse and clearance center was always busy.

Every detail was thought out and no area was neglected. Some of our vendors marveled over the carpeting and fine shelving and fixtures in a warehouse that also held moderately priced and clearance merchandise. However, this held true to our philosophy about treating customers well, no matter what their budgets. Not to mention that many wealthy customers visited the third floor to stock their beach homes.

Sadly, as our business grew, my mother's health continued to decline. My brother and brother-in-law were both doctors and treated her, but her circulatory problems became so severe that it was necessary for one of her legs to be amputated. Of course, this made it impossible for her to do much at the shop. In a horrific twist of fate, my father had been diagnosed with cancer. He still ran Jacobson Produce. However, as he became more ill, it was becoming more difficult for him to keep the business going.

When it became clear that my mother's circulation in her remaining leg was becoming more of a problem, she made plans to go to Houston, Texas to a vascular surgeon who thought he could save her remaining leg. Before she left in fall of 1966, she told me that she has to speak to me. She confided that if she lost her remaining leg, she would not be coming back to be an invalid. She also told me that the medical care that both she and my father had needed had sapped their assets. They had only $1,000 in the bank, and the gift shop as assets, as Jacobson Produce had not been a significant source of income for some time. I could see how pained she was that all of her years of hard work hadn't made her able to leave my siblings and me a sizeable inheritance. When it comes to illness and family, you have to be clear about your priorities. Seeing her so sad about everything was very difficult, as was the realization that my mother's body was failing her more every day.

"Mom, you raised me to be a responsible person. You gave me my education. You helped me build this store. That's more than a parent owes a child," I told her.

Then, she grew more serious.

"I taught you how to run this store," she said. "I expect you to keep it going."

I knew how much the store meant to her and I intended to do just that.

As sick as my father was, she didn't want to worry him and simply told him that she was going to be fitted for a prosthetic leg. We said "goodbye" and she flew to Texas. My sister and I took turns visiting her over the next several weeks, as my father was too ill to travel. Shortly after she left, her remaining leg was amputated. It was November when my mother called me from Texas. She told me about the surgery. It was the last time that I spoke with her. She died a few days later. Less than two weeks later, my father lost his battle with cancer.

The tragedy of burying two parents 12 days apart was a sharp contrast to the busy and festive time of year. It was December, and we still needed to serve our customers during this busy month. I did the best I could, wearing a smile for the customers, but it was a very sad time for all of us.

There was wild speculation that the store would close without my mother. She was well-known and beloved, and many thought that I didn't know how the store operated. What few realized was that I had been running things for years as her body slowly deteriorated. I knew the store inside and out. I developed the manufacturer relationships and chose the inventory and provided the highest level of service to the customers. I knew the store's operations better than she did and, because of my youth, I had been the one doing most of the leg work, as well as the research and buying for the store for years.

However, upon reading the will, there was a problem. My parents left the store equally to me and to my younger sister. My older brother was a successful doctor and my older sister was married to another successful doctor, so I suspect that they wanted to be sure that my younger sister was cared for through the assets of the store. This put me back in the position of one store supporting two families, with two owners making decisions. If I couldn't run the store on my own, it wouldn't be possible to continue it.

After consulting an appraiser, I found that the building was worth approximately $40,000—less than the amount that was owed on it. I went to my sister and explained my situation. Since there were no liquid assets left from my parents and the store had acquired significant debt from the expansion, it would be impossible for the store to split its profits two ways. Any money that the store made still needed to be reinvested back into the business. The only option we really had was to sell the business and pay off the debt.

My sister had watched how hard my mother and I had worked to build the store over the years. Her life had taken her in a different direction and she didn't have an interest in running the store. In an incredibly generous move, she signed over her shares of the store to me. I was the sole owner of Brielle Galleries. Many years later, after the store blossomed, I was able to compensate her for her generosity.

I finally had the ability to realize my vision for the store. I knew that we needed to make a dramatic change in order for it to become the premier retail location for luxury goods in the area. First, we needed to change how the store looked to our customers—obtaining more visibility.

I decided to add a two-story façade to the store. When I explained my plan to my accountant and attorney, they both said I was crazy. They thought that I should continue to expand the back of the store; that a space 13 ½ feet wide by 59 ½ feet long added to the front would do me no good—not to mention that building such a relatively narrow area two stories high wasn't typically what a retailer would do. Getting people to go onto a second floor of a store is generally more difficult than getting them to browse the first floor. They both strongly urged me to reconsider, but I knew what I wanted to do.

I had established a good track record paying back the original loan, so I was able to take out a second loan of $50,000. With that began the construction of a dramatic new façade. The new front of the building was designed almost entirely in glass and we had two elegant spiral staircases that led up to the second floor. Of course, this required tearing apart the store again. Fortunately, we had enough repeat business that we were able to keep traffic coming in during the four-month renovation.

The result was what I had ever imagined: A beautiful, two-story, glittering storefront that was befitting what we had created inside. But the large, tinted windows weren't the only part of my plan.

After we landed Lenox, we were able to attract other high-end brands, including Waterford, the famous Irish crystal. I had created a Waterford room and had cultivated a fantastic relationship with the company, whose American headquarters was coincidentally based a few towns away. Our sales were doing well enough that I felt that I could call in a favor.

I went to visit one of my contacts at the company, John Miller, the company president. He had been the top crystal buyer at B. Altman in New York and then went on to become the president of Waterford USA. I knew that they had no less than 50 large chandeliers in the warehouse a few miles from my store.

"Here's what I want to do," I told him. "You give me seven of the chandeliers you have in inventory. I'll take them on consignment. Every time I sell one of them, I'll pay you for two."

In exchange for that deal, I would give his chandeliers premier placement in our new façade, which could be seen for a mile away. Our stretch of road was pitch black at night, and I was creating a building with a Fifth-Avenue look. He saw what I was trying to do and gave me the lighting that I needed to make a real impact.

I also knew that the American artist Edna Hibel had developed an incredible following for her lithographs, prints and paintings. I invested in some and hung nearly 70 lithographs and prints by Hibel and by other artists on the walls of the balcony, so that they were visible from the road at night.

We were fortunate that our architect, who designed the façade, was extremely talented, as well as knowledgeable about developments in new building materials. Had been a friend of my mother's and took great care in designing our building. When he suggested that we install large back-lit panels on the front of the building that would light up and elegantly showcase the products we carried, I knew that he understood exactly what we were trying to do. He found the perfect material from which to make the signs from manufacturer Rohm & Haas. Each large lighted panel was a deep blue with white letters that named our products: china, crystal, jewelry, silver.

The chandeliers glittered, highlighting the beautiful prints on the walls. The signage could be seen from both directions, above the bridge to our south and at the traffic light to our north. The store looked magnificent to those who passed by. During the times when the Brielle Bridge was raised to let those massive yachts and fishing boats into the inlet, cars were backed up in front of the store for 5 to 10 minutes, with nothing to look at except see the magnificent spectacle that we had created. I set all of the front-store lighting on a timer that illuminated them at dusk and kept them running until 11 p.m., giving us tremendous visibility for hours after darkness settled over the area.

A comparable billboard near our location would have cost us $10,000 to $12,000 per year. Our store, once an eyesore, was now one of our greatest marketing assets—enhanced by seven chandeliers and a captive audience—promoting Brielle Galleries well into the evening hours, long after we were closed. The beautiful spectacle attracted many new customers who returned in the days after they first drove by the store in the evening. They had to see the interior for themselves.

One day, a man who was spending the summer in nearby Bay Head stopped into the store and remarked about the blue panels, asking where we had purchased them. I explained that they were from Rohm & Haas, a

Ira's Business Rules

Make the Most of What You Have

I could have made the decision to move the store, but it was an asset that the business owned outright. It didn't make sense to incur a mortgage or rental expenses, especially when we had already invested so much time and expense in our expansions and our fixtures. So, it made more sense to make the most of what I had.

By enhancing the front of the store, against the counsel of our legal and financial advisors, I was able to create a stunning new showplace that was attractive to customers and turned out to be a great marketing tool. So, it's important to look at what might be the perceived weaknesses in your business and find ways to turn them into strengths. Many times, you can do this without abandoning what you've already built.

maker of building materials used in signs. The man was shocked—he was the president of Rohm & Haas. He told me that we were one of the first customers to use this new type of material.

The following year, the store's revenue doubled. It took less than 12 months to recoup the investment in the storefront. When I met with him to review our books, my accountant apologized to me for doubting my vision. The expansion had clearly paid off.

CHAPTER 5

Moving Forward

It was the beginning of a new era for Brielle Galleries. We had new bills to pay, and I worked on getting our name out there as much as I could.

My uncle owned a newspaper in Detroit and helped me decide how to market the store. He came up with the slogan, "We take the 'if' out of gift," which we used in our early advertising.

With the summer crowds at the shore, it was becoming very popular to hire small planes to fly advertising banners along the shoreline. I decided to put the slogan on a banner and give it a try. On Wednesdays and Saturdays, when the weather was nice, the planes would fly out of Lakewood to the beach in Mantoloking, then north along the Jersey shore to historic Monmouth Park, a well-known horse racing track in Oceanport, about 20 miles north. After flying twice around the track, they would head south again. It was estimated that, on the most crowded days, they reached more than 500,000 people, all relaxing and having a great time, for a mere $300 per flight, weather permitting. If the day was grey or rainy, the planes wouldn't fly since no crowds would be out and about anyway.

People visited our location, believing that the airplane was our own—and a shop wealthy enough to fly its own airplane along the shore must certainly have some fine items. This helped us get the attention of many customers.

I had also started going on the road to teach people about the products that we carried. From exclusive women's clubs to tiny garden clubs, Helene and I hauled china, crystal and silverware to meet with all sorts of groups. It didn't matter who the group was—if they asked me to come, I went to talk about our products. Once, I set a full formal table for eight on the second floor of a tiny firehouse in Farmingdale, New Jersey—a town that measures one square mile.

These meetings never failed to bring new faces into the galleries. Because we had always worked hard to be inclusive of our customers—we literally had something for everyone and welcomed someone with a $30 budget as warmly as someone with a $3,000 budget—Brielle Galleries became a favorite with many different people in the area. They talked favorably about us and the word of mouth began to pay off.

The head of a northern New Jersey Catholic school used to come down to the shore during the summer. Sister Corita visited Brielle Galleries whenever she was in town to see what we had on display. She loved crystal and the porcelain figurines.

One day, she turned to me and said, "You know, Ira. These things are fabulous, but I don't understand anything about them—how they're made, why they cost what they cost."

It was December and we were busy, but I offered to walk her through and explain the items to her, and she agreed. I started talking about these things that I had grown to love. I explained how the porcelain molds may take months to create, and how the tiniest imperfection or unexpected variation in firing can cause a delicate piece to shatter into hundreds of pieces. I explained how crystal is hand-cut to perfection, and how craftspeople spend countless hours perfecting their work to make the beautiful pieces of art in the galleries.

As I spoke, I became more passionate about each item. It was important to me that people understand that these were not just pretty plates and knick-knacks. I wanted them to understand the artistry behind the piece. I wanted them to understand that a $500 bone china plate isn't just a more expensive version of a $5 earthenware dish. So, I shared the details that I had come to learn over years of working with these products.

As I spoke to Sister Corita that day, I noticed that a few people had gathered and followed us around the displays, listening to me speak. By the time we finished, more than a dozen customers had joined us on the impromptu tour. After the customers left that day, Helene, who had watched the whole thing, pulled me aside.

"Ira, you need to teach this," she said.

"What do you mean, teach this?" I asked.

"You need to take an hour out of your day and teach people. They see this beauty but they don't understand it. Once they understand it, they want it," she said.

"But I don't have time," I replied.

"You'd better make time," she said. She emphasized that American porcelain figurines were an art form made here in New Jersey. It was quickly becoming our most important product line. We should be the experts teaching people about it.

Once again, Helene was right. Every day at 2 p.m, I started giving a tour to explain the items in the galleries. We didn't advertise it beyond putting a sign on the first floor, but word of mouth soon took over. Within a few months, we had to set a maximum of 25 people because that was the amount that we could accommodate in the various galleries. A friend of mine owned an engineering firm nearby and one day his wife called me. She had a group of 25 people coming in from India as part of the renowned People to People program. Would I give them a tour? Of course, I told her. The group was wowed by what they saw, and I continued to get letters from many of them for years.

The tours proved again that our philosophy of creating a destination that had something for everyone was exactly right. One afternoon, I had an exclusive women's group that was scheduled to tour the galleries. In walked a man dressed very casually in shorts and a t-shirt. He browsed around, then asked if he could join the tour. It would have been easy to dismiss him, but I would never do that, so I told him he was welcome to join us. Afterwards, this well-known doctor from Illinois purchased a series of porcelain Cybis Native American figurines for $20,000. This reinforced to me that you can't judge a book by its cover.

By this time, our daughter, Lisa, was about 13 years old. She was a lovely, precocious girl, and had been spending time at Brielle Galleries since she was a baby, and had grown up surrounded by the products we carried. She had listened to me give the tour countless times.

One day, she asked me if she could run the tour. She was barely a teenager, but I was so busy that I welcomed the extra hour to get things done. People were so delighted that this young girl was so poised and well-versed in our products that our young tour guide was an instant hit. From that point on, Lisa periodically gave tours when she wasn't in school.

In addition the tours helped our customers expand their tastes. Some were Cybis collectors, others loved Waterford. The tour allowed us to show them new fine items about which they may not know. By exposing them to our inventory and explaining the craftsmanship, many of our customers became collectors of many types of fine porcelain, crystal, silver and other pieces of *objets d'art.*

After offering the tour for several months, I realized that my explanations could only communicate so much. People needed to see the processes that created these works of art. I decided to put film facilities into one of the galleries, inserting a motorized screen that could be lowered during the presentations and retracted at other times. I purchased a projector and folding, accordion-style doors for one of the galleries. After all, if a picture was worth a thousand words, then a short film would be priceless.

In the middle of the day, after the tours, I turned out the lights and showed two 17-minute professionally produced films about how the Cybis and Boehm sculptures were made. There was no audio, so I narrated it, explaining the techniques used for making porcelain. Once again, many of my dealers thought I was crazy to turn off the lights and block off valuable floor space in the middle of the day. But people flocked to us to see the film. Both the film and the tour were opportunities to personally introduce people to the products. I could see to which products they were drawn and which left them lukewarm. After some time, I could get to know clients better and would almost always guess the products they would love. We kept files on their purchases to help us notify customers when new pieces came in. It helped me get to know my customers and my products better, and it ended up being an important selling opportunity for us.

The sales came in unexpected ways. I also gave lectures to a class of the local elementary school that visited the gallery. The children were delighted to see how clay could be made into these magnificent sculptures and how crystal could be carved to have such brilliant designs. One year, shortly before Mother's Day, a young boy of about 12 or 13 came into the galleries. He had ridden his bike and his cheeks were a bit flushed and his hair tousled.

"May I help you, young man?" I asked him.

"Yes, I'd like to buy this for my mother," he replied.

He pointed to a small Cybis sculpture of Eros, the god of love. I explained to him that the sculpture was $325. He said that he knew that. It was a good bit of money for a young boy to spend, but he told me that he had sat through one of my lectures at the gallery and thought that the sculpture would be a perfect Mother's Day gift for his mother. He had saved since the lecture and finally had enough to buy it for her.

I happily sold it to him, ensuring that it was wrapped perfectly and that he would easily and securely be able to carry it on his bicycle. After all, any young person who showed enough resolve to save and purchase such a wonderful gift for his mother deserved as much respect as one of the top collectors we serviced.

The tour had become so important to us, and allowed us to reach several thousand people over the course of the few years it was offered. However, the tour could only accommodate 25 or so people per day. Of course, some customers couldn't make it to our location at the time, and

Ira's Business Rules

Educate Your Customers

Sales experts might tell you that you should always be trying to sell your customers. But I've always believed that they need to understand your products and services first so that they understand the value that you're delivering to them.

I integrated an education component into virtually everything we did. I made sure our floor staff was always well-trained in the products they represented. We invited representatives from all of our top manufacturers to come in and give our staff presentations on the product, so they were always versed in the latest that was happening with Steuben, Buccellati, Boehm, Cybis, Baccarat, Lalique, Waterford and the other brands that we carried.

The tours and the films helped customers understand the many hours of training and the artistry that went into our products, as well as the level of quality and taste that they represented. Even when a young bride-to-be came into our shop to choose her china pattern, I tried to help her understand what she was choosing and to think about what she would like five or 10 years ahead.

Nurture your customers and help them understand their needs and how you can help. That's the best way to earn trust and loyalty over the long run.

we were increasingly doing business over longer distances. Customers who came to visit from out of town would later order from us by phone. And there were some who just weren't interested in or able to come in for the tour or film.

I had to find another way to reach them.

I created the "Brielle Galleries Porcelain Report." This simple, four-page newsletter updated customers on our latest porcelain offerings and gave them useful information to help them understand the product. The newsletter was just two-color, but we included photographs to show customers the products. Our first run was 1979 and was sent to our existing mailing list—approximately 1,000 people. It also gave us a wonderful way to keep in touch with our customers and teach them more about the products they were purchasing. This was a great way to position Brielle Galleries as a key source of information; an expert as well as a retailer.

As I looked at the list to which we were mailing the report, I began to realize something amazing. Our customer base was now well beyond the borders of central New Jersey. We were seeing orders come in from states further and further away. More and more people were seeking out the not-so-little shop under the bridge in Brielle.

CHAPTER 6

Finding the Right People

The galleries were gaining a substantial client base—one that needed personalized attention to cultivate. Once, the head of a Fortune 100 company visited us, wanting to replace his entire crystal, china and sterling silver flatware service. We had been apprised of his arrival by his interior designer, who was a regular client of ours. That day, in a move that was out of character for me, I dressed in a suit. I introduced myself as the president of the gallery and then disappeared to let my employees help him with his purchases.

We had worked with his designer to set seven different tables of china, crystal and silver. After the CEO glanced around, he asked to be left to look around for an hour. Almost exactly 60 minutes later, he placed an order for 18 new place settings of Flora Danica, our most expensive, exclusive and unusual pattern which was imported from Denmark, as well as all of the accompanying accessories, flatware and crystal. He ordered three other sets of new place settings, as well, for a total of $350,000 worth of merchandise.

Fulfillment was always something at which we excelled. I had all of his merchandise ready and, within a week, I was at his door, personally overseeing the delivery. My assistant and I unpacked, checked, and cleaned

60 place settings, then stocked his cabinets with the new merchandise. The CEO arrived home just as we were finishing the job. He seemed surprised, since the last time he saw me, I was wearing a suit and presented to him as the president and CEO of Brielle Galleries.

"What are you doing here?" he inquired. "I didn't expect you."

I explained that it was important to me to personally oversee our larger clients to ensure their satisfaction. The CEO grinned and said, self-confidently, "I'll bet that this is the largest sale you've ever had."

His face fell a little when I told him it wasn't. But the truth was that clients were finding out about us and becoming loyal, repeat customers. He invited us to have dinner with him. As we dined, he asked if I had brought the Buccellati catalog with me. Of course, I had—as well as a variety of other catalogs. After our meal, he placed an order for an additional $70,000 worth of silver accessories. Later, he spread the word to two other Fortune 100 CEOs, who each purchased tens of thousands of dollars of merchandise from us for their companies, as well as their apartments in Manhattan and their summer homes in the Hamptons and Palm Beach. Clearly, my personal touch had made a big difference.

Such adventures were exciting, but it soon became clear that I couldn't do this on my own. We needed to keep track of our clients and their preferences. We kept records on their previous purchases so that we could alert them when new products that would be of interest to them arrived. We needed more specialists who could properly service our exclusive clientele.

However, I also had to be very selective about the people I hired. Many of my customers were highly accomplished professionals who collected the very best of everything. Not only did they expect us to give them the exceptional attention that they were used to receiving elsewhere in their lives, they expected my staff to be knowledgeable in the many intricacies of the pieces that we sold. So, the people who worked with customers needed to be carefully screened and trained.

Brielle Galleries had been built on a foundation of inclusiveness. While retailers often try to serve niche markets, we tried to have something for everyone. And, regardless of whether a customer walked into our store with a $25 budget or a $25,000 budget, I insisted that they be treated with the same level of respect and professionalism.

There were some boutiques where the staff had to address the owner as Mr. or Mrs. and others where, if you didn't speak multiple languages and dress in expensive designer clothes, they wouldn't give you the time of day. Well, I learned early that attracting many customers with varying budgets was a better strategy than serving a few who might move or otherwise go away. Not to mention that you could never judge a book by its cover. More than a few times, a customer wearing an old trench coat or a t-shirt and blue jeans turned out to be a wealthy collector. I recall one evening when a man came into the galleries at closing. From the way he was dressed, he looked like he was someone of very modest means. I was alone with only one other employee, who was helping me close up. We waited for the man to finish shopping, and he surprised us by purchasing a $1,000 piece of porcelain art. He asked that it be delivered to his home. I oversaw the delivery myself and was shocked to see five gold records on his wall. Who were we to judge the way that our customers dressed?

Over the years, we had hundreds of salespeople who were required to learn all about the various product lines. If they had familiarity with the products, as well as the poise to handle our customers appropriately, they went on the main floor. Some of our younger salespeople needed training and worked their way up from the wrap room to the selling floor. By that time, they were well-versed in our products and could converse about them with anyone. They were friendly, enthusiastic and adhered to our mission of "service above all else."

There were some stars among the employees, though; some people who were integral to our success. One of those people walked into the store in 1968. Eleanor Kuta was the wife of a dentist who had moved his practice from northern New Jersey to the shore area. Mistaking us for a furniture store, she came in to look for chairs for her husband's dental practice which, unfortunately, we didn't carry.

As I spoke with her, I saw that her effusive energy was engaging. This was someone very special. I was taken with her sense of style and taste, and I knew my customers would be, too. I'd never been shy about taking calculated chances, so I offered her a job on the spot, telling her that if she ever decided to come work for me, there would be a job for her. I'm not sure why I thought she would accept. She didn't need to work. And I certainly couldn't pay her a vast sum of money, as most of our cash was tied up in our inventory. But I just had a sense that she would be a good fit.

It was more than a year later when she walked back into Brielle Galleries and accepted my offer, almost instantly becoming a critical part of the business. She and her secretary worked at modest, bare-bones desks set up at the back of the warehouse. Hardly posh surroundings, but we always did what we had to do in those days. Eleanor was extremely down-to-earth and didn't really care about her workspace. On the other hand, she cared deeply about how the galleries looked and operated.

At first, she oversaw the porcelain art gallery. When she helped customers, she had a warm manner and a way of making it seem like they were the most important people in the world. Soon, it became clear that she had a flair for merchandising and design, so she began taking on more of those responsibilities. Her impeccable taste made such a difference, and she brought unique touches to everything we did. During the evenings, she created hand-sewn tablecloths for our displays and events because she was very particular about how they should look. In fact, at one of our famous merchandise shows, a representative of Tiffany asked me who designed our display tables. I told him that we had a remarkable employee who did them. He said that they were better than the ones at his legendary boutique.

Several years later, I came across another unexpected gem. I received a phone call from George Barker, the vice-president of Boehm. He told me that Ray Blackman, a top porcelain marketer at the famed gallery Reese Palley in Atlantic City, New Jersey was leaving to take a sales job in Pomona, California. However, Ray was the most successful Boehm marketer in the United States, and Helen Boehm was concerned because the strongest part of her market was in the northeastern part of the country. If he went to California, the company stood to lose a significant portion of its sales.

George asked me if I would offer Ray a job. I had serious reservations about whether I could afford him or not. However, if he was as good as his reputation indicated, I knew he would be a tremendous asset to our business. At the time when we hired him, we were the number-one dealer of Cybis porcelain in the country. A smaller studio than Boehm, Cybis specialized in creating human figures, where Boehm's strength was birds, flowers, and animals. Having him represent Boehm for us would help us expand our ability to reach new markets. In addition, our wide variety of crystal, silver, and other luxury pieces gave him a wider array of products to sell to his clients. After some negotiating back and forth, we came to an agreement and Ray came to work for our business in 1979.

It wasn't long before Ray developed the nickname "The Pied Piper of Porcelain." He had a tremendous following of porcelain enthusiasts, and they were very loyal to him. I had known about Ray long before he came to work for us because people would visit us, but refuse to buy product from us, as they would only buy from Ray. He knew how to romance a product like no one I had ever seen. He took every customer seriously and studied their interests.

A few days after he came to work for me, he approached me about giving him a "promotion" to vice-president.

"Ira, my customers don't want to deal with a salesman," he said. "Give me the title vice-president so that we can say that they're being personally serviced by the vice-president of the company."

This made sense to me, so I changed his title. He suggested that we send out an announcement letter about him joining the company, including his new title. That single letter sold nearly $40,000 worth of product. Everything he touched, when it came to porcelain art, sold.

Ray had been doing business on a national basis regularly and knew exactly how to service our high-end customers. For larger sales, he would deliver the product personally, sometimes flying cross-country, to ensure that the piece arrived intact. He would set it up himself, ensuring that the proper fixtures had been purchased and assembled correctly. Customers were very impressed by how seriously he took their purchases. So much so, in fact, that they remained loyal to him above all others. Customers would come to our gallery and fall in love with a piece, but they wouldn't buy it from me—they insisted on dealing with Ray. At least now they were still buying it from Brielle Galleries instead of purchasing it from another store where Ray worked.

If the customer was close enough, he would pack up special pieces into a van and travel, with a driver, to deliver porcelain to customers. He would also note other customers on his route and bring extra porcelains so that he could stop and visit them to show them our new offerings. He always chose the product carefully, bringing only those which he thought they would love.

Eventually, Ray was writing fully 20 percent of the sales of the business. He was so knowledgeable about porcelain he was retained as an expert to testify about the value of the porcelain collections owned by couples who were divorcing. Often, we found that collectors didn't fight about money as much as they argued over who would get the porcelain figurine collection.

Ray also cultivated a highly successful business segment dealing with insurance companies, finding replacements for pieces that had been destroyed or stolen. Since many of these pieces were rare limited editions, replacement wasn't always easy. However, when a piece was broken or stolen, most people wanted to replace it instead of collecting the insurance money. Ray seemed to have a gift for finding and acquiring exactly the right piece, and insurers came to rely on him. It was an unexpected, but profitable, part of our business.

The third jewel in the Brielle Galleries crown also came through Boehm. Carolyn Langdon had applied to be an artist at the Boehm gallery. A graduate of Rosemont College, she was a brilliant marketer, and Helen Boehm recognized her talents, hiring her to work in marketing and sales. Through my dealings with the studio, I had become acquainted with her and was so impressed at her ethical nature, intelligence and warm personality that I knew she would be a wonderful employee. However, Helen Boehm was such a good friend that hiring Carolyn away from Boehm was unthinkable.

Several years later, Carolyn had found it was time to pursue new opportunities. She interviewed at other luxury goods manufacturers and word got back to me that she was looking for a job. I reached out to her and offered her a position with Brielle Galleries, marketing and selling our porcelains and other fine goods. She accepted and became part of our team in 1979.

Ray preferred to work independently as the head of marketing. So, I began to look for other opportunities in the business for Carolyn's talents. At the time, we had a fledgling corporate department. She was a dynamo with some terrific contacts and some great ideas for growing that area, so I put her in charge of that division.

Carolyn's philosophy about service matched my own. She began contacting prospects and developing customers among regional businesses. One of our clients was the Monmouth Park Racetrack, a historic horse racing facility in Oceanport, New Jersey. While it might have seemed odd to purchase trophies from a gift and china shop, the creations that Carolyn oversaw were unlike anything that could be purchased elsewhere. Many of the track owners and managers were tired of the silver plates that had been standard issue for so many years. Horse owners were bored with receiving the same old trophies.

Instead, Carolyn took samples of Waterford vases and attached them to rich wood bases, engraved with winners' names, customized horse-themed vases and other unique products. They were worlds apart from the standard silver plates and the like that could be purchased from traditional award shops.

Much of the track management saw the purchase and fulfillment of trophies as a headache—one of the details of their business that was important, but time-consuming. So, when they became confident in Carolyn's ability to provide unique products quickly, much to the delight of the owners and trainers who ran their horses at the tracks, they would purchase large quantities, perhaps a six-month supply or more. They would notify us with the race winners, which set us on our own race to consistently deliver the trophies quickly and accurately.

Where other providers took four or five weeks to deliver engraved goods to clients, our order fulfillment took about five days. One shocked horse owner called me to express his amazement, saying that he had never received his trophies in less than several months after the event. We had delivered it to him within one week. Eventually, we were servicing most of the major racetracks on the east coast.

No one could figure out how we did it, but the answer wasn't a great mystery. We had developed some business contacts, who worked with us, but who became good friends. Carolyn found one local man, a retiree, who had been a hand engraver for Tiffany. He still had the equipment in his garage, and agreed to take on work for us. Of course, his skills were excellent and he gave us fast service because we paid him immediately upon completion of his work for us.

When we would get an order, someone—usually me—would drive it to the engraver who would begin engraving immediately. Then, we would pack the trophy or cup the same day and send it out. Soon, the word got out among race tracks on the east coast. The extra level of service that we provided landed us a large network of new customers.

Carolyn had a knack for dealing with corporate customers and grew that division to be a significant portion of our revenue. She, along with Eleanor and Ray, exhibited incredible dedication to the business. They all worked until the job was done and took their roles in Brielle Galleries very personally. They became friends, as well as colleagues, and stood by me throughout the time that I ran the business.

Ruth Paperth was another employee for whom I found a job, and who became an important part of our success. She was a local customer. Lovely and glamorous, she had been a model for Lux Soap in her youth.

While Ruth knew jewelry, she wasn't a gemologist, but I knew she was the right person to head up our new jewelry department. She had a knack for helping our customers choose exactly the right pieces and for selecting inventory that she knew customers would love. I was right. Within a few years, Ruth had grown our jewelry revenue to $400,000 per year.

All of our employees put in long hours, working weekends during events and doing whatever it took to keep the galleries running smoothly. While I couldn't pay them high wages, I did what I could to make the environment happy and fun. I made sure that employees who were sick weren't financially devastated by their maladies. Many of the employees became good friends, holding parties at each others' homes and otherwise socializing in their off-hours.

There was no pretense in the galleries—everyone called me "Ira," and I was more likely to take out the garbage as anyone else. In fact, some of my employees called the Dumpster my office because I made so many trips out there. But I always believed that I couldn't ask my employees to do something that I wasn't willing to do. I recognized employees when they went above and beyond the call of their jobs, and I tried to create an environment that felt like a family. Very few employees ever left that family.

In addition to the employees who worked so faithfully for us, we had a network of suppliers and service providers who were invested in our success. A great example of this was William "Billy" George, who eventually took over the helm of Waterford. He had seen what we were doing with the galleries and approached me to find out how he could help Brielle Galleries sell more of his product. He believed we could be selling much more.

Having exclusive lead time, a period where a product was only sold through our business before it was released to other retailers, was always good for our business, giving us the ability to offer something that no other retailer had. Waterford was also willing to give us an exclusive on a beautiful crystal sea horse that we helped develop for the cover of our

Ira's Business Rules

Your People Make Your Business

The most successful people surround themselves with smart, talented colleagues. Without people like Eleanor, Ray, Carolyn and Ruth, my business wouldn't have been nearly as diverse and fast-growing as it was. They provided insight, creativity, dedication and talent, and were willing to do whatever it took to make the business successful. Not one of them was hired through a newspaper classified ad or through an executive recruiter. I found the people before I had places for them in my business. But you'd better believe that I made room for them when I found them.

It's been said so often that it has become a cliché, but people are your greatest asset. They bring ideas and ingenuity. They'll tell you what you're doing right and tell you what they think could be done better. And if you treat them well and provide a great working environment, you'll have the benefits of their talents and expertise for years to come. My key employees delivered nearly a century's worth of experience to Brielle Galleries.

catalog. We sold 10 limited-edition sculptures at $5,000 and more than 800 of the non-limited sculptures at $185.

Our reputation for fast fulfillment was important to us, so having our orders prioritized was essential. He agreed to help us attain all of these things, in addition to allowing me to pick up product directly from the warehouse, just two towns away. That kind of support and relationship building helped us increase our Waterford sales from $18,000 per year to $935,000 per year in just three years.

Our success came from our core principle of valuing people—whether they were our employees, our customers, our suppliers or our community members—and building relationships. When you cultivate meaningful business relationships with these groups, who understand your vision, they become committed to helping you succeed.

CHAPTER 7

Strength in Numbers

The fate of my business was inextricably tied to the growing strength of the porcelain figurine market at the time. There had always been a market among young affluent women who received sets of china as wedding gifts. However, there was a new movement in the porcelain art industry. More collectors were becoming passionate about figurines and sculptures crafted in porcelain. And I found my shop in the middle of a movement that was fast gaining momentum.

The development of porcelain heralds back to Chinese dynasties from more than two millennia ago. Former Boehm president Frank Cosentino documented the history of porcelain in his book *The Boehm Journey to Ching-te-Chen, China, Birthplace of Porcelain*. The history of hard-paste porcelain dates back to the Han Dynasty in China 206 B.C. In the late 13th century, Marco Polo brought back the first samples of fine ceramics fired at high temperatures. For many years, Western artisans tried to recreate the fine, translucent material that heralded from the Orient, but they lacked knowledge of the proper firing techniques and ingredients to do so.

To understand the intricacy and artistry in the porcelain figurines we carried, it is necessary to understand a bit about porcelain itself. There are three types of porcelain: hard paste, soft paste, and bone china. Hard paste is fired at very high temperatures and the clay ingredients fuse together into a very hard material. Soft paste is fired at lower temperatures and has a granular feel. It is easier to break apart, since the materials do not fuse together, and must be glazed. It is used primarily for lower-end plates, dishes and some sculpture, but its consistency makes it difficult to achieve fine detail. Bone china is very translucent and strong, fired at high temperatures. Its composition includes bone ash added to china clay. As far as finishes, the European market had a strong preference for glazed pieces, which had a deep shine, while Americans tended to prefer the bisque finish, with its more matte appearance.

Hard-paste ceramics fall into three categories: First, there is earthenware, which is made from lower-grade clays, then stoneware, which is similar to earthenware. Stoneware clays include materials like feldspar, which fuses the material, and is fired at temperatures around 2000° Fahrenheit. The result is a stronger, whiter piece of ceramic.

The finest form of hard-paste ceramic is porcelain, which is a more translucent form of stoneware fired at much higher temperatures. The porcelain mixture is poured into plaster molds that were created from an original sculpture and left to set. The plaster molds draw moisture from the mixture; the longer it is left to set, the thicker the porcelain. After 10 minutes, the clay would be approximately 1/8-inch thick—perfect for firing. The pieces are then attached with a clay mixture called "slip," and fired at temperatures of approximately 2400° Fahrenheit.

Once each piece is removed from its mold, it needs to be supported in order to be fired. The supports, or props, that hold the piece in place are created out of the same clay, preventing it from slumping or falling apart during firing. Since each piece reduces in size approximately 12 percent during the firing process, the props that are assembled to hold each piece of the sculpture in place during firing have to be made of the same material. If the props differ in content from the sculpture, they will not reduce at the same rate, resulting in disfigurement or shattering during the firing process. One edition of a porcelain sculpture could take as long as six months or more from initial concept to mold creation to pouring the sculptures, then firing, painting and finishing them.

While U.S. porcelain production started in earnest in the 1950s, it caught on as a major trend among collectors in the 1970s. There were a number of factors driving the growing porcelain market at this time. First, this was a new U.S. art form, with porcelain studios like Cybis and Boehm the first to create hard-paste porcelain figurines in this country. The beauty and intricacy of these pieces made them an immediate hit among collectors. They marveled at the pieces, which were at once incredibly strong, and beautifully intricate. American-made porcelain was getting a reputation for quality, great artistry and, of course, the cachet of having been made in the U.S.A., which was of great importance to many people at the time. In addition, national advertising programs were fueling demand across the country.

Also, at that time, interest rates were climbing to near 20 percent. With inflation so high and the value of the U.S. dollar so weak, collectors were buying anything they could that might have intrinsic value, or which might appreciate in value, to preserve their wealth. Auction houses like Sotheby's and Christie's thrived. Porcelain from artisan studios like Cybis and Boehm was catching on and the demand grew. Collectors would reserve one of a limited number of pieces, sometimes waiting as much as a year or more to receive their treasures.

In the 18th century, porcelain making was finally perfected in Europe, and England eventually became an important center of porcelain artistry. In the late 18th and 19th centuries, famous porcelain makers like Meissen, Dresden, Minton, Rockingham, Coalport and Royal Doulton began.

Porcelain making began in the 18th century in America, but the figurine market didn't catch on in full-force until the 20th century. In 1949, a small porcelain studio named for the Polish-born porcelain sculptor Boleslaw Cybis opened in Trenton, New Jersey. Cybis, the son of the chief architect of the Czarina's summer palace at St. Petersburg, had arrived in the U.S. to paint murals in the Polish Pavilion at the 1939 World's Fair. Cybis applied for American citizenship for him and his family and his famed work in Poland began to gain a following in the United States. He eventually settled in Trenton. I never knew him, however. I dealt primarily with Marilyn Charlton, the brilliant artist who took over the studio when Cybis died. She and her husband, Joe, were the driving forces behind the growth of the company in later years.

In the early years, Cybis made a wide variety of porcelain sculptures, eventually specializing in human figurines, a form in which the company's artisans excelled. They could capture the emotion on a human face or the curve of a hand in perfect detail. They soon became one of the favored porcelain makers among collectors.

In 1950, Boehm Studios also opened in Trenton, featuring the exquisite birds and flowers sculpted by American artist Edward Marshall Boehm. Edward had a spectacular aviary where he kept his rare birds and flowers from all over the world to use as models for his incredible sculptures. He had a true gift for modeling sculptures and each had extremely fine detail that made it life-like. His wife, Helen, a dynamic personality with exceptional business acumen, kept the pieces in limited distribution, enhancing their value among collectors.

At first blush, New Jersey's capital city, Trenton, may seem like an unlikely location for two of the world's finest porcelain studios. The venerable china house, Lenox, was founded there in 1889 by Walter Scott Lenox. The city offered easy transportation options, as well as proximity, to New York City and Philadelphia. Clay could easily be shipped in from all over the country, giving the more than 200 19th century porcelain and pottery producers ample resources with which to work. So, Cybis and Boehm were a natural fit for the area.

There were also brilliant artists in the porcelain studios in England. In later years, one of the most accomplished would be Connoisseur. Formed by a contingent of artisans from Royal Worcester, including Diane Lewis, a flower modeler trained by the famed porcelain artist Dorothy Doughty, who became the world's best, as well as some of the artisans from Boehm's England studio. The studio had an incredible group of clay modelers and

Ira's Business Rules

Keep Your Eye on the Trends

No one could have predicted what a popular art form porcelain would become in the United States. While I recognized the quality of the pieces I sold, it was a combination of effective merchandising and market conditions that helped position many of the luxury goods that we sold, such as to take off the way that they did.

In our case, we were an integral part of creating the trend. There were a number of factors that contributed to the demand for porcelain art. Ray had developed an incredible following of collectors who purchased from us. The Reese Palley gallery, located near key convention venues in Atlantic City, attracted the attention of affluent travelers—doctors, attorneys, business people and other professionals—who visited the area for their conferences. We launched a new national advertising campaign at the same time that our "Porcelain Report" newsletter was gaining in popularity. These promotional elements, along with an expanding customer base of influential collectors of porcelain art, were the driving force behind the growth of the market.

The lesson here is to pay attention to market conditions and recognize emerging customer preferences. A few hints at the beginning of an upswing can yield tremendous results if you respond to them.

designers. We took almost all of their production and this became an important exclusive product line for us nationally in later years.

As our customer base expanded beyond New Jersey's borders, it became imperative for us to have a more national perspective. Eleanor, Carolyn, and I began traveling to shows in Atlanta, Dallas, and Los Angeles, as well as New York, to look for the latest trends and influences in the markets. Regional nuances were difficult to master, but also very important. We found that many collectors in the southern U.S. preferred more traditional pieces, while contemporary flair was more valued in markets like Los Angeles. We even traveled to luxury goods shows in Frankfurt, Germany which gave us a wonderful global perspective which wasn't readily available in the days before the Internet.

Eventually, we became so good at delivering customer insight that some of our studios would seek our advice and even made special commissions and limited editions for Brielle Galleries. We were the only luxury retailer in the country that was showcasing these beautiful pieces in individual galleries, creating a spectacle that was unlike anything outside of their own studios. As a result, we quickly gained favor with the studios, which appreciated the attention to and elegant presentation of their work. Our customers loved the galleries because they were like museums—we mixed $300 pieces with $25,000 pieces. They could see the range of art that was available. We added early museum pieces for clients to see pieces that were not available for sale. Our customers loved this, and our competitors tried to copy what we were doing.

We even worked with studios on special projects. In 1973, I was planning a trip to Israel, with my daughter, Lisa. When the management of Burgues Porcelain found out about the trip, they asked me to take a porcelain sculpture of a sabra cactus flower, which is also the country's national flower, to the then-President of Israel, Zalman Shazar. The flower had special meaning because the word sabra also refers to someone born in Israel.

I wasn't comfortable making a presentation to a head of state as an ordinary citizen. I believed that the proper protocol should be that the piece be given as a gift of state, so I contacted the U.S. State Department, and they agreed. The State Department worked with the Israeli government to make the arrangements. The sabra was packed carefully in a burnished walnut case. It traveled in the airplane cabin with us so that we could ensure it arrived safely. When we got to Tel Aviv, we were picked up by a black Cadillac and whisked off to the new Presidential home in Jerusalem, which had been recently completed, where we met with the President himself. Bestowing the gift on behalf of my country felt like the right thing to do.

He marveled at the beauty of the sculpture. While we thought that this was going to go to the Jerusalem museum, he was so touched by the gift that he insisted that it stay in his personal residence. He invited two of his bodyguards in to see the piece. Seeing their emotional reaction to this symbolic piece was a reminder that the beautiful objects that we carried were also rich with personal meaning and relevance.

Some products were added to our lines as a result of customer requests. When a young woman came into the shop and asked for Buccellati silver, I had never heard of it. But you had better believe that I got on a train and went to New York to check it out. Once I saw the exquisite pieces, we added both their flatware and holloware lines to the mix, eventually building an exquisite gallery that housed the largest presentation of Buccellati silver in the country. My friend, Anna Vardalla, who was part of Buccellati's staff and whom I believe to be the greatest expert in sterling flatware and holloware, praised our marketing expertise and unusual gallery, comparing them to top retailers in the U.S. That type of feedback made me realize how far we had come—and that we were doing all the right things to grow the gallery.

After we landed Lenox, we were able to get most of the other lines that we wanted. With the exception of one luxury good retailer with locations in West Orange and Bay Head, we really had no competition in our geographic market. So, we were able to qualify for most lines without worrying that the territory was protected. Many of our primary manufacturers—Waterford, Boehm, Lenox, Cybis, and others—were located in New Jersey, giving us an important advantage. In many cases, I was able to negotiate with them so that we could go directly to manufacturing headquarters and pick up the merchandise, which saved us significant shipping costs and time in fulfillment. Also, in the case of Waterford, we were the only dealer able to gain access to the warehouse, which was nearby.

This access was critical at high volume times, such as the December holidays. While most retailers had received all of their merchandise by December 1, we were able to gain access to the warehouse any time up until the afternoon of December 23, when they closed the warehouse for the holiday. So, we didn't have to worry about running out of product, like many other retailers did. If one of our corporate clients needed 50 to 100 or more vases a week before Christmas, we could deliver in one day.

Like our corporate engraving service, this type of fulfillment capability set us apart from any competition. Sure—you could get a Waterford bowl at a department store—as long as they had it in stock. However, it was unlikely that you would be able to get large numbers of them, packaged, wrapped and shipped to arrive in a matter of days. Once again, our location—as well as our creative business approach—was paying off.

CHAPTER 8

The Next Level

With a growing staff, Ray overseeing our consumer sales and Carolyn spearheading our corporate division, I was able to once again focus on the overall direction of the business.

The store had taken most of my time. Helene and I had two young children; Lisa, born in 1959, and Daniel, born in 1961. While they were young, Helene left working at the store to care for them. During the evenings, I would take a break for a couple of hours and meet the three of them at the nearby beachfront burger stand. We would eat hamburgers or sandwiches from a little stand and then spend an hour playing on the beach or just watching the waves roll in. This was an early attempt at work-life balance, which is so important, and kept our family close. So, even though I was working long hours, the children later said that it felt like I was around more than I was. For that, I will always be grateful to Helene.

Inside the store, the various rooms and galleries made it look more like a museum than a specialty retail shop. Many often referred to Brielle Galleries as "a museum with price tags." I made it a point to feature an array of products from affordable to ultra-expensive to show people the wide range of creations from the various brands that we carried. In our Lalique gallery, for example, I had a $35,000 crystal table that we had fixed to the floor and lit from underneath. It was located in the exact center of the store, and the result was a breathtaking display that drew attention from all areas of the store. Even the people from Lalique were impressed. And, of course, there was a psychological factor: Next to a $35,000 table, a vase that costs $1,800 doesn't seem as expensive!

By the early 1970s, our children were in school and Helene came back to work at the store. She was concerned that having the owner's wife

Ira's Business Rules

Family First

It is very easy to let a business consume your life. There is always something that needs your attention, some new detail to which you need to attend. Along with increasing profits and hiring staff, you need to make your family and your personal life a priority, as well.

Clichés often become clichés for a reason—because there's truth to them. However, without a base of people who love and support you, success—or life, for that matter—has little meaning. As you grow your venture, find ways to involve your family. Helene eventually came back to work for the store. Lisa and Danny worked there part-time, helping customers, and wrapping gifts. This allowed us to be together as a family, even as I was working. Meeting the customers and seeing the business that I was building, first-hand, also gave them an appreciation for the business that took so much of my time.

The bottom line is: No matter how successful you become, don't forget your family along the way.

work on the floor would be disruptive and intimidating to many of the employees who had so rigorously trained for floor sales positions. Using the creativity that was such an inspiration to me throughout our marriage, she looked at the areas that the business could better service, and decided to launch a special orders division.

Often, we would have customers whose china or silverware patterns had been discontinued and who needed to replace lost or broken pieces. Helene became an expert in tracking down these hard-to-find items, much to the delight of customers. We became so well-known for our ability to replace discontinued items that large department stores would routinely refer their customers to us for replacement items. This became an important source of referral business for us, even though these massive retailers didn't realize it. Once customers saw our level of quality and service, and were delighted by our ability to replace their beloved pattern pieces, they often shopped with our store rather than the large, impersonal department stores.

Even as we grew, we continually ran into one challenge: A shortage of fine porcelain figurines. We became the top seller of Cybis and Boehm porcelain in the country, yet we could not keep enough stock to satisfy demand. Since the highly coveted pieces were made in very limited quantities, we often sold out of our allotment even before the pieces came into the store. Such a shortage of inventory meant lost revenue for my business. Even as we expanded our product lines, adding sculptures by the artist Gunther Granget and the popular and more mass-market Lladró porcelains, we often found ourselves unable to meet demand, even though we took on virtually every appropriate line that we could find. These included Laszlo Ispanky, Doris Lindner, Dorothy Doughty and others of equal artistry and quality.

It was the late '70s when I decided to try to rectify this myself. With Ray as a business partner, we recruited two talented English porcelain specialists. Brian Omerod was a master sculptor who created incredible clay models. Simon Joyner was a painter of fine porcelain. I wanted to create porcelains that were different from what was already on the market. We opened the doors to the country's newest porcelain studio—Bronn of America—in a small house a block away from the store. The name was a combination of Brian and Simon's names.

The two primary centers of porcelain production were, at the time, the eastern United States and England. Each had a distinct style of porcelain production, which was especially evident in the painting. American painters were typically "stipplers," using a brush called a "deer-foot," because of its v-shape which resembled a deer's hoof. It allowed the painters to soften the color, but the result was a somewhat uneven effect. European porcelain painters typically used a "badger brush," made out of that animal's fur, which gave a more even and uniform coat to the piece. Bronn's creations were representative of Americana, especially of western themes, but reflected a distinctly European style of painting to differentiate itself from other American porcelain studios.

Bronn's creations were high-end—none of our pieces retailed for less than $1,000. Our most renowned piece, the Wolf Hunter was a $7,500 piece of which only 15 were made. Within a year, the piece was no longer available at retail, having been sold out, but was re-selling in the secondary market—where collectors re-sell to other collectors—for $12,500.

These larger pieces were much more dramatic—and much harder to produce. A massive kiln was housed in the garage of the house, where the artists also lived on the second floor. It could take six months to create a limited edition of a sculpture; an exhaustive process of sculpting clay and then dissecting the piece to create molds. If the clay was not separated in exactly the right manner, the porcelain mixture poured into the molds would slip out or not fire correctly, and all of that work would be lost.

Once the pieces were created, they needed to be re-attached with a substance called slip—a porcelain mixture—and were held together by props created from the same material as the sculpture. The pieces were then fired again to create a hard, solid piece of surprising strength. A piece would routinely reduce in size approximately 12 percent between the stage of being wet clay and being completely fired and solid, and if there was a tiny bubble or crack in the thin, 1/8-inch porcelain, it might shatter into hundreds of pieces during firing, dashing dozens of hours of work. Approximately 5 percent of every firing was lost to breakage in the kilns. Each sculpture was reproduced in a small, pre-determined quantity, after which the molds were destroyed to ensure the exclusivity of the creation.

The result of all of this painstaking effort was another incredible boost to our business. Having the Bronn studio did two things for us: First, it gave us a collection of western-themed art, which was popular at the time. In addition, having the studio so close to our store, made it easy to bring customers over to show exactly how these incredible pieces were made. None of the larger studios would allow customers to tour because they were concerned that it would distract the artisans from their work. In addition, there was always a concern about breakage of the fine pieces.

Inviting our customers to the studio proved to be a huge advantage for us. Once a customer saw that creating fine porcelain was far more than just making a mold and filling it time and time again; that it took infinite artistry and patience to sculpt the initial piece, which was then destroyed to make molds, and that the molding process was nearly as intricate as the sculpting, they had new appreciation for why the sculptures were priced as they were. The demand was so high that half or more of each sculpture quantity was sold out before its introduction. Most of the rest was committed before the next show at Brielle Galleries.

Meanwhile, in the store itself, we began to host events to create more traffic and excitement. In one of our first events, we hosted a show of silver Churchill commemorative plates from Silver Creations, Ltd of Emerson, New Jersey. The plates were introduced by Sarah Churchill, the daughter of British Prime Minister Sir Winston Churchill, who autographed each certificate of authenticity. We sent out invitations to our customers and placed a few ads in local newspapers. I thought it would be an enjoyable day for our customers and, perhaps, drive up our sales a bit.

On the day of the event, I was shocked by what I saw. The store was packed and there were lines out the door to meet the daughter of such a legendary leader. Throughout her entire time with us, Miss Churchill was busy meeting and greeting customers, who were delighted to shake hands and purchase the pieces she represented. We sold more than 50 plates at $150 each.

The Churchill event showed me that by bringing in celebrities to meet and greet our customers, we could create more demand for our products. And what better way to create a store for everyone than to have our day-to-day customers rubbing elbows with the rich and famous? I began to plan ways to bring a bit of Hollywood—as well as Washington and Broadway—to Brielle.

Ira's Business Rules

A Gold Brick is Just a Brick

I've often said that even a gold brick is just a brick unless you market it properly. By creating an air of glamour, but keeping our down-to-earth approach to people, we were able to create excitement about the products that we carried. Our store became a destination—people traveled to see the incredible pieces we carried. However, these weren't one-of-a-kind antiques. They were usually items that people could get elsewhere. So, by creating an air of uniqueness—offering the beauty and service and speed they couldn't get elsewhere—we were able to sell our gold bricks quite successfully.

CHAPTER 9

The Shows and Giving Back

After the success of the Sarah Churchill show, I knew that I had to find a way to bring even more glamour and excitement to the store. The Churchill event showed me that even though people thought of our store as a destination, an event with special guests and exciting products would bring in even more traffic. And since giving back to the community had always been a very important part of our business, it was a natural fit that we created a philanthropic element to these events.

We always supported local charities. In fact, I don't believe that I ever turned down a request for a donation in the 50 years we were in business. Brielle Galleries donated pieces for auctions and fundraisers to benefit local causes, such as the Arthritis Foundation, the Monmouth Park Charity Fund and local hospitals, schools, and houses of worship.

In the early 1970s when we began staging events at the store, we always kept charity as our focus. Actually, the events were staged outside the store, where we converted our relatively small parking lot into a luxurious tented addition to the store. Here, Eleanor's creative wizardry was a driving force in planning celebrations that became the talk of the retail industry nationwide.

Our first major event was the opening of the Cybis gallery in the back of the store. We brought in extra product and invited our customers into the store. We served hors d'oeuvres and cocktails. It was a huge success, but the gallery was too small to house the many people who wanted to attend. So, when we planned our second show, several months later, we added a tent on our parking lot. For that show, we created an auction, and the Cybis studio painted some of the lower-priced pieces as one-of-a-kind productions. The collectors went mad over these little porcelain sculptures that would never be produced again. A piece that usually sold for $125 would easily sell for $500 when it was recreated in this way. Such limited editions added to the air of excitement and exclusivity of the event.

Word-of-mouth became our best marketing for the shows. People told their friends and neighbors and, eventually, these events came to reflect the entire philosophy of our store. They were open to everyone—you might find millionaires and celebrities chatting and mingling with people of considerably more modest means. Everyone ate together and enjoyed the entertainment and joyful atmosphere, always to benefit a charitable cause.

Many of the events were themed around a particular product line or an element that I had dreamed up. In 1979, we hosted an event to introduce the Cybis porcelain Medieval Chess set. Inspired by the 14th century Nine Heroes tapestry, which hangs in New York's Metropolitan Museum of Art, each chess piece was decorated in sapphire blue with highlights of 14-carat gold and was approximately seven inches tall. In the middle of a tent in our parking lot, we displayed the set, which sold for $30,000. It was the same chess set that had been a gift from the President of the United States to the Russian Premier earlier that year.

To celebrate the event and add that celebrity element that our customers loved, chess master Arthur Bisguier of the U.S. Chess Federation played 20 matches simultaneously with our guests, winning every single one of them within 30 minutes. I never saw a group of people so happy to lose.

The studios with whom we worked were so impressed by the sudden popularity of the shows and pulled out all of the stops to support us. We did a Lladró-themed show, and they sent two tractor trailers filled with more product valued at a million dollars wholesale, plus 10 employees to help us run the event and manage the merchandise. We introduced an exclusive nurse figurine that had been developed specifically for the event. The night before the event, Señor José Lladró signed 300 individual pieces, which were then carefully repackaged in their boxes and stacked in the warehouse. We sold every single piece. At another show, Buccellati sent armed guards and jewelry valued at more than a few million dollars for a show. They had never done such an event before, or since, that was such a wild success.

One of our most memorable events was a mock horse race for the Monmouth Park Charity Fund, which was affiliated with the renowned area horseracing track. Eleanor painted colorful, miniature wooden horses. People placed mock wagers on the horses and cheered like mad for their little wooden horses as they circled around the track, moving as many spaces as a wheel-of-fortune dictated each time it was spun. Monmouth Park sent its professional announcer, who called the race as if there were live thoroughbreds rounding the track, and a famous jockey was there to mingle with the crowd. That event netted $10,000 for the charity.

Once, when Eleanor was browsing through an issue of *New York* magazine, she noticed a story about a Sumo wrestler and his wife who owned the best sushi restaurant in New York City. The idea led to a fantastic show with a Saturday night celebratory dinner of authentic Japanese food, and real Sumo wrestlers who wrestled in a match in our tent during the event the following day to introduce a new Connoisseur porcelain collection with Asian themes.

In 1979, we hosted an event that featured the Boehm Tutankhamun series—porcelain replicas of the famed collection—in an event which benefited the Monmouth Museum. We hired mimes who were painted gold, turning them into stunning life-size figures representing the Egyptian king, Tut. They didn't move a muscle as they stood there. As people watched, fascinated by the skill and discipline of these live statues, the curtains parted and a sedan chair, carried by several large men, entered the tent. Out came a belly dancer, who entertained the crowd, much to their delight.

Celebrities were also a big part of the events. We also hosted an event to benefit the Cousteau Society, with Jean-Michel Cousteau, son of the famed marine explorer Jacques Cousteau. He signed copies of his book, and sold more copies than he had ever sold at any event in their history. This was one of our most successful shows, attracting more than 3,000 people. For this event, Cybis created a humpback whale sculpture, of which we sold 18 in one afternoon. A portion of the proceeds went to the Cousteau Society.

At one event, the actor Tony Randall was given an award by Cybis for his work with the Theatre Museum for the City of New York. He was familiar with the area where our store was located because he had been in the service and had been stationed at nearby Fort Monmouth for part of the time. Helene took him on a tour of our store. As he walked around, he noticed the elaborate hors d'oeuvres being passed around and the four bars stocked with top-shelf liquors. When he saw me, he asked, "Who's paying for all of this?"

"I am," I replied. "But I'll let you pay for it if you like."

He laughed and shook his head and said, "No, thank you." He was a bit incredulous at the fantastic spread.

But, the truth was that we spared no expense when it came to these events. Eleanor was able to spend whatever she needed to make the events successful. Sometimes, the bills for two-day shows topped $100,000. While it was important to break even, I knew that if we did the event well that the money would flow, so I never restricted spending, and every show made money. The biggest risk that we ran was rain—a downpour could quickly ruin our well-laid plans. However, our ace electrician, Bob

Sauer had taken on more and more responsibility from show to show, soon becoming our operations manager for these events. He always had contingency plans. He had shuttle buses on stand-by in case we needed to have people parked in nearby paved areas. We could then transport them through the rain with minimal discomfort.

I knew that these shows represented more than the sales that we made on-site. They were a combination of entertainment, sales, food and socializing. People were eventually clamoring to get into the events. We had to limit the number of customers who could attend, often sending invitations to those collectors of the product lines we would feature, or only to our very best customers. This gave people incentive to purchase from us. Doing so gave them an exclusive benefit: Entrance to our shows. However, we didn't mind so-called "crashers," who came with invited guests. If a regular customer with an invitation brought a few more people to the event, we certainly weren't going to turn them away. Chances were that the people they brought with them had similar taste and interest in fine goods, so they were likely to become our customers as well.

In order to get people into the store so that they could see the rest of our products, we placed two bars indoors. One of the bars was placed directly next to the jewelry case in the front of the store. This was strategic—as people waited for their drinks, they shopped for jewelry. Our vendors would bring in millions of dollars worth of rings, necklaces, bracelets and other beautiful pieces on consignment, and provide their personnel to sell to the crowds. It was common for customers to walk around showing off a bracelet or ring she had just picked up while waiting for a glass of wine or soda.

One of our most cherished relationships was with Very Special Arts, the nonprofit that helps children with physical and mental disabilities learn through, participate in, and enjoy the arts. It was founded in 1974 by Ambassador Jean Kennedy Smith, and is an affiliate of the John F. Kennedy Center for the Performing Arts.

We were introduced to the organization, which is now called VSA Arts, through our friend, the artist Edna Hibel, who was working on a project for them at the time. Their mission to foster appreciation of and to provide greater access to the arts was so completely in line with our vision for Brielle Galleries, that it was a perfect fit. It also allowed us to expand

Ira's Business Rules

Marry Your Customer to You

Our shows gave us a great opportunity to set ourselves apart from the competition, offering something that no one else could. They were glamorous and fun, and our customers loved to feel like they were part of an exclusive club when they got their invitations. Attendees came from approximately 20 states and five different countries.

When you have a business, it's important to continually find ways which make your customers remember why they choose you as their service or product provider beyond all other businesses. What can you offer that no one else can? The shows, along with the exclusivity of our product selection, our legendary service, fulfillment, knowledge and attention to detail were all parts of a package that made us stand out from other providers who may have been more convenient.

As you consider your business, look for what your clients would love for you to do for them. Be creative and think beyond the norm. Our shows, for example, were beyond what anyone else in the industry was doing at the time. They thrilled our customers and kept them coming back to us time and again.

our philanthropy to the national scene. I spoke with the executive director at the time, Eugene (Gene) Maillard.

In total, we held three fundraising events for Very Special Arts. Since the organization was so well-connected with artists and political figures, it attracted celebrities and luminaries from all over the country. Helene and I were invited to an event at the Kennedy Center, which included an exhibition of art from the Very Special Arts program, to thank us for the work we had done for the charity. During the performance, we were seated in the box next to the Kennedy and Shriver families. It was a delightful surprise when she invited us to join her for a reception at Ethel Kennedy's farm in Virginia. As we walked into the beautiful home, we were suddenly surrounded by celebrities like Crystal Gayle, Lauren Bacall, Lou Gossett, Jr. and many others. It was great fun to be treated like royalty for the evening.

For Boehm's and Brielle Galleries' 40th anniversaries in the spring of 1990, we held a lavish ball at the Berkeley Carteret hotel in Asbury Park. For the event, Helen Boehm collaborated with socialite and entrepreneur Georgette Mosbacher to create a special series of porcelain flacons for her perfume, One Perfect Rose, which was produced by La Prairie. Mrs. Jehan Sadat, widow of the late Anwar Sadat, was also a guest, invited by her friend, Helen Boehm. Mrs. Sadat was a visiting professor at the University of Maryland at the time, and made the trip up to our event at Helen's request. She was being honored with the creation of a beautiful Boehm porcelain, "Jehan Sadat Blue Nile Rose."

At the time, Asbury Park had fallen on difficult times and was faced with a rising crime rate. Even so, we thought that bringing such a lavish event to the once-thriving resort town would be a great way to bring publicity to it and to help spur its revival.

Georgette's helicopter landed on the lawn in front of the hotel, and she was ushered into the ballroom in grand style. Our customers loved mingling with Georgette, Helen Boehm, and Mrs. Sadat, as well as Governor

James Florio and his wife, Lucinda. The next day, in the store, we had a rose-draped station inside where Georgette stood and greeted guests, sharing samples of her perfume. She was due back in Washington, D.C. later that evening, but didn't want to leave Brielle Galleries, because she was having so much fun.

Of course, such extravaganzas aren't without their glitches. At one of our early shows, Eleanor constructed a miniature carousel. Our trusted electrician and all-around logistics manager, Bob Sauer, who worked miracles during our events, was called in because the carousel turned—backwards. What could have been an embarrassing faux pas turned into a delightful tale of disaster averted. The very few times we did have rain on the days of our events, it was generally not torrential, and people came out to the events in spite of the dampness.

In the store, everything was perfect. I'll admit that it wasn't unusual for me to get a brainstorm about how to re-merchandise some element of the store the night before a big event. I often spent the entire 24 hours before one of our shows at the store, working on both the perfection of the tented area and the store itself.

The shows were held twice a year, once in May and once in November. For our November shows, we would be sure that the store was beautifully decorated for the holidays. Eleanor would order new ornaments and decorations every year, creating new themes and color combinations. No one ever saw the same holiday décor twice at our store, and our decorations became their own attraction after the shows were over.

Word spread about our shows and how lavish they were, we started attracting more and more people. At the first event in the Cybis gallery, we had a few hundred people. After that, we never had fewer than 1,500 people at an event, and at the four most popular events, we had more than 3,000 people. This could have been a big problem for our little store, especially since we were using the parking lot as exhibit and seating space. However, this was where our ties to the community also came in handy.

For years, our store had been building business in Brielle. We invited students from the school next door to seminars on porcelain art at the shop. We always did what we could for local charities and the town. So, when we needed extra parking, the township and the school opened up their adjoining parking lots to us, allowing us ample room to park the 800 or so cars that traveled from all over the state and beyond to come to the show. They always went out of their way for us, just as we had for them. Again, this is where building relationships helps business in ways that cannot be foreseen.

We also catered the air of exclusivity in our invitations. People would plan their vacations and their business travel around our spring and fall shows. Our invitations were always lovely and professionally printed, with directions on how to get to the store from the airport, from local marinas where customers could dock their yachts, and the like. We also offered to arrange for a car service if they were traveling from far away to attend.

Over the years, we had 41 shows at Brielle Galleries. The events became the hallmark of who we were as a company, setting us apart and helping us build a name that resonated nationally.

Ira Jacobson, age 17, in the U.S. Navy.

Tillie Jacobson in the store's early days.

Building a Brielle Galleries storefront that would rival any Fifth Avenue boutique.

From left: Pierre Matisse, Eleanor Kuta, and Alan Gershwin at a dinner honoring Ira Jacobson and his friend, restaurateur Joe Amiel.

The Brielle Galleries staff would regularly get together and socialize.

From left: At a Cybis show, Joseph and Marilyn Chorlton, owners of Cybis; Jean Wrightson, philanthropist and part of the family that owned A&P supermarkets; Ira Jacobson; Marie White, co-founder of the Monmouth Park Charity Fund.

Mrs. Emlen Roosevelt; Ira Jacobson; Lisa Jacobson; and Emlen Roosevelt, Theodore Roosevelt's nephew at the first Brielle Galleries outdoor event.

Carolyn Langdon holding a Boehm bird.

Luca Buccellati, owner of Buccellati Silver at Brielle Galleries' Buccellati show.

A Master Engraver of Waterford Crystal carves his signature on a piece he designed during a Brielle Galleries event.

Spanish Flamenco dancers provide entertainment at a Lladró show at Brielle Galleries.

Maestro Alfredo Silipigni, of the New Jersey State Opera and his wife, Gloria; Tony Randall and Helene Jacobson at a Brielle Galleries event that benefited the Theatre Museum for the City of New York.

Lord Piers Wedgwood at a Waterford-Wedgwood event at Brielle Galleries.

Helene Jacobson; Lucinda Robb, Lynda Johnson Robb, daughter of President Lyndon B. Johnson; artist Edna Hibel; and Ira Jacobson at a Brielle Galleries show for the National Archives.

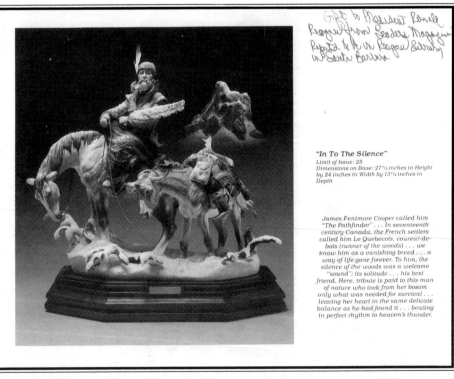

"In To The Silence"
Limit of Issue: 25
Dimensions on Base: 27½ inches in Height by 24 inches in Width by 13½ inches in Depth

James Fenimore Cooper called him "The Pathfinder"... In seventeenth century Canada, the French settlers called him Le Quebecois, coureur-de-bois (runner of the woods)... we know him as a vanishing breed... a way of life gone forever. To him, the silence of the woods was a welcome "sound"; its solitude... his best friend. Here, tribute is paid to this man of nature who took from her bosom only what was needed for survival... leaving her heart in the same delicate balance as he had found it... beating in perfect rhythm to heaven's thunder.

Bronn porcelain sculpture, "Into the Silence," which was given as a gift to President Ronald Reagan by Leaders *magazine.*

Helene Jacobson at a fundraiser at the Garden State Arts Center.

Family portrait, from left, Ira, Lisa, Dan, and Helene Jacobson.

From left, Lucinda and Governor James Florio; Helen Boehm; and Mrs. Jehan Sadat at the 40th anniversary celebration for Boehm and Brielle Galleries. (1990)

Georgette Mosbacher and Helene Jacobson with Helene's parents, Dr. and Mrs. Kalmen Motiuk at a Brielle Galleries event. (1990)

*A spectacular perfume flacon produced by Boehm for Georgette Mosbacher's
perfume, One Perfect Rose.*

The gorgeous interior of Brielle Galleries.

Restaurateur Joe Amiel and actor Danny Aiello at Monmouth Park Charity fundraiser.

Hillary Clinton receives the Theo Fabergé White House egg, a gift from the Congressional Club at the annual First Ladies Luncheon. (2000)

Ira Jacobson and President Zalman Shazar of Israel at the presentation of the porcelain sculpture at the President's new home in Jerusalem. (1972)

OFFICE OF THE PRESIDENT OF ISRAEL   לשכת נשיא המדינה

Jerusalem, 18 July 1972

Mr. Ira Jacobson
Brielle China and Gifts
Highway 71
Brielle, New Jersey 08730

Dear Mr. Jacobson,

I trust that you and your lovely little daughter enjoyed your tour of Israel and your trip home. For our part,
in the Residence of the President of Israel, we remember
your visit with undiminished pleasure, reminded as we are
by the exquisite Prickly Pear Cactus that now adorns the
house and delights the eyes of so many observers.

President Shazar has asked me to convey his great
personal appreciation to you, the bringer, and through you
to the masterly artist, Dr. Burgues. We are indebted to
him not only for the loveliness of his creation but also
for the thoughtfulness which led him to present his cactus
to this land of the cactus.

Cordially,

Shulamit Nardi
Shulamit Nardi
Assistant to the President

N.B. Under separate cover we are sending you a few photographs taken during your presentation of the Cactus.

SHN/MB

Presentation of a donation to New York Police and Fire Widows' and Children's Benefit Fund at Gracie Mansion with Mayor Michael R. Bloomberg and baseball great Rusty Staub in attendance. (2003)

Crystal sculpture made in honor of 9/11 by Waterford artisans.

Opera singer Jerome Hines performs on the Brielle Galleries parking lot.

The Steuben gallery at Brielle Galleries—one of the select Steuben dealers in the country—designed by the Steuben architect.

CHAPTER 10

Aida

About 30 miles north of our location was a wonderful open-air ampitheater called the Garden State Arts Center. In 1968, the arts center opened on Holmdel's Telegraph Hill as a center of culture and recreation. In the decades that followed, before it was leased by a for-profit entity in the 1990s, the programming included a number of classical and popular acts. Part of the arts center was the Garden State Arts Center Cultural Fund, which provided free entertainment each year to school children, senior citizens, blind people, mentally challenged people, and disabled veterans. It was entirely supported by donations as a way to give back to the community.

Several circumstances created the perfect opportunity for the grandest production that the Arts Center ever saw. First, each year, the Garden State Arts Center would hold a gala to raise money for the Cultural Fund to kick off its season. They were lavish affairs, and the invitees were the who's who of New Jersey society. In 1977, Maestro Alfredo Silipigni of the New Jersey State Opera wanted to create a glamorous and sophisticated following of his opera company throughout the state. His vision was to elevate the New Jersey State Opera to the level of the great opera companies in New York and Philadelphia. The previous year, Silipigni had staged "La Traviata" by Giuseppe Verdi at the Arts Center, which was attended by more than 6,000 people. He wanted to create another operatic production in Holmdel.

At the same time, the Arts Center leadership, including New Jersey Highway Authority Vice-Chairman Robert J. Jablonski was thinking about how the facility could expand the future of the classics in New Jersey. Coincidentally, 1977 was also the Arts Center's 10th anniversary, the perfect occasion to do something very special.

So, when Maestro Silipigni approached the Arts Center about staging the grandest of all operas—Guiseppi Verdi's "Aida"—which would star the famed opera singer Robert Merrill, the idea was met with nothing less than an enthusiastic response. Aida's powerful story and stunning visuals of ancient Egypt would be a production never seen before in the Garden State.

Of course, staging Aida is no easy feat—it includes marching armies, moving sphinxes, and even an elephant. Performers would include the New Jersey State Opera and the New Jersey Ballet. Even two local high school bands were involved for additional musical support.

One of the biggest patrons of the Arts Center was my customer and friend Patricia Kelly. The wife of the executive of a large construction company, she was the epitome of grace and glamour. She was also a generous philanthropist, and giving back to the community was a common interest of ours.

She had been named the chairperson of the entire event and called me one day during the early stages of planning the opera. In conjunction with Silipigni's company, the Arts Center was planning its fundraising gala—and it needed a gala chairman. She asked me if I would fill the role, overseeing the gala and its committee. She and I discussed how the event would take shape. I had a perfect idea: Boehm had created the Opera Rose, a beautiful pink porcelain rose sculpture. I suggested that Brielle Galleries create an exhibition of Boehm porcelain on the night of the gala.

It would be the largest such exhibition ever of its kind. Over the next several months, I worked with the Arts Center and the New Jersey Opera to create an outstanding event to raise money for the Cultural Fund.

As planning and creation of the production itself got underway, there was an incredible amount of excitement surrounding it. The New Jersey State Council on the Arts donated $15,000 toward the production costs and agreed to use the opera as the kick-off to their own summer festival. Helen Boehm was the honorary co-chair, and the public relations was being handled by Letitia Baldrige, former White House social secretary to Jacqueline Kennedy.

Of course, I was aware of the event's plan, and had already spoken to Helen Boehm about it when I got a phone call from Mr. Jablonski. His private secretary had been a fan of the shows at Brielle Galleries, and he had a reason behind his call.

"Ira, I need you to sponsor the opera," he said. "It will cost you $40,000."

My heart skipped a beat as I tried to do the math in my head. There was no way we would be able to afford such an expense!

"Commissioner . . . " I paused. "There's just no way I can do that."

He let out a laugh that indicated he had been joking. "I know. But if you'll do the tent decorations for the gala, you can do a display of your pieces on the grounds."

He suggested putting our display in the north parking lot, which was where the gala patrons were. I objected. I wanted everyone to have access to our display, which would be the largest exhibition of Boehm porcelain ever assembled. So, we were put in an area of the grounds where we had to work around nearly two dozen trees. It didn't matter.

Our product display was one of the largest events that we ever took on outside of our own shows. We worked with Letitia, providing her with some of our press contacts. However, a conflict with her schedule arose and she was unable to ultimately handle the public relations. She called me and apologized, in the gracious way that one would expect from the world's foremost expert on social graces. She apologized for not being able to complete the engagement. But, of course, we had handled PR before with our many shows.

Several weeks before the event, I received the opportunity to give back in a much more personal way. A letter arrived at the store. It was handwritten, from the daughter of a cobbler in New York City. An Italian immigrant of modest means, he had made his way to the United States decades before to create a better future for himself. While wealth eluded him, through the years, two things remained constant in this life: His love of the opera Aida and his devotion to his wife, Rose. So, when he heard about the production of Aida and the exhibition of Boehm's Opera Rose, he was elated.

Of course, he did not have the financial wherewithal to actually attend. Instead, he had his daughter write me that lovely letter explaining the situation and thanking me for being a part of this event, which meant so much to him. I immediately took the letter to the Commissioner and asked for three of the best seats in the house. I got them. I contacted the women who had written the letter and told her that her father would, indeed, be attending the event.

With a tear in his eye, the opera-loving cobbler; his wife, Rose; and the daughter who wrote the lovely letter on his behalf would all attend the event. The story was picked up by New York's *Daily News*, which ran a 2/3-page story. On the day that it ran, I got a phone call from Letitia congratulating me on the great press for the event. Now, that's a compliment!

The days before the event were a flurry of non-stop work. The exhibition was housed in a series of large tents near the venue, with four varied garden areas, each featuring different products. Eleanor had found a large Bonsai tree and affixed small platforms to it. On each was an exquisite Boehm bird. The Bonsai was placed in a small pond that we created, in

80

which there was also a pair of beautiful porcelain swans. A sound system with bird calls made it seem as if the birds had come to life and were singing for us. Another exhibit depicted the arid desert with a beautiful porcelain roadrunner. And, of course, a special exhibit dedicated to Boehm's opera rose.

The opera itself was magnificent. The scenery was designed by Robert Yodice, resident designer for Manhattan's famed Julliard School. At only 20 years old, he had to design a set that would be flexible and interchangeable enough to maneuver all of the elaborate changes within the constraints of the Arts Center's stage. He created one set featuring a monumental Sphinx whose head alone was 20 feet high.

At both intermissions, there were long lines to enter the tent. I was amused to see that the Brielle Galleries philosophy was being played out in those lines. As I looked down the long row of people, I saw David Sarnoff, chairman of NBC, and opera star Anna Moffo waiting alongside lawn-seat ticket holders. No one got preferential treatment—everyone was treated equally.

At about 11 p.m., the show was about to wind down, and many of my employees wanted to go home. I didn't often put my foot down, but this time I did. We would stay until after the performance was finished and until everyone who wanted to see the display had done so. The tent didn't clear out until after midnight.

In a way, that meant our work had just begun all over again. Since Jerome Hines was coming to the galleries the next day, we had invited nearly 500 of our VIP customers to see and hear him sing. There was a great deal of preparation to be done. We needed to move all of the Boehm sculptures—both ours and those that Helen Boehm had lent to us for the event, back to the gallery. We needed to move fixtures, boxes and tent decorations based on the Opera Rose. It took all night, but by mid-morning, the store looked like its sparkling self.

The next day, Jerome Hines arrived at Brielle Galleries. He was impressed by the display, but retreated to one of our offices to ensure that he would not be called upon to speak too much and strain his voice. An hour or so later, he was on the blacktop, his powerful bass voice overwhelming us with its beauty. Having such a world-renowned opera singer entertain some of my best customers in our little parking lot was a moment I'll never forget.

Ira's Business Rules

Learn to Negotiate

There's a business adage that says that you know a negotiation has gone well when both parties walk away slightly unhappy. I don't believe that. I think that the best negotiations meet the needs of both parties. But you can't be afraid to ask for what you want or what you need. It took a bit of nerve to ask a world-famous opera singer like Jerome Hines to sing in my parking lot. But I knew that I had something of value that the gala and production needed—my ability to stage my own successful events.

Ask for what you want. The worst anyone can say is "no." And more often than you think, you'll get more than you need.

CHAPTER 11

From Regional to National

I f the shows built our reputation through word-of-mouth, it was our advertising program that made us known nationally.

Initially, we advertised locally. Of course, we had the airplane banner ads, and we also did a bit of local newspaper advertising featuring various products. In addition, we had a mailing list which we used for our catalog and to invite customers to our shows. Radio was also a key medium and I recorded the spots myself. My staff insisted on that, saying that people knew me as the voice of the galleries.

As our shows grew, Eleanor created a long list of media who attended press conferences. Sometimes, we would have 25 or so media representatives on hand to see Ruth Warwick, who starred in *Citizen Kane*, Tony Randall, or Kathryn Crosby, who appeared at our shows. The combination of celebrities and beautiful products never failed to make newspaper headlines.

Probably our most successful in-store promotion was our beautiful wrapping. We offered free wrapping for every gift, no matter what the price. Our wraps were elaborate and our hand-made bows were crafted out of various types of ribbons and other materials. The wrapping was so special that it became another reason that people shopped at our store—to have their gifts adorned so beautifully. People began to purchase items from us just to be sure that they would have the stunning wrapping on the distinctive box from our store. As our name became more recognized, our packaging became as important to us as Tiffany's blue box is to them.

We were always looking for ways to reach broader audiences, however. It was in the mid-1970s when Frank Redden, a director of Cybis, made me an offer that would become another piece of the puzzle of our success. He approached me about launching a national advertising campaign in Connoisseur magazine, an upscale lifestyle publication. He made an interesting offer: I would pay for the advertisement, featuring their product as well as Brielle Galleries. He would give me enough porcelain figurines to offset the cost of the ad. To sweeten the deal, they would give us an additional quantity of limited edition porcelain to sell, adding value beyond the cost of the advertisement.

For other retailers, that offer may not have been advantageous. After all, we would be shelling out cash, and reimbursed in product. For us, it was exactly what we needed. We were hungry for more porcelain art beyond the allotment that the studios gave us. We routinely sold out of those allotments and had huge waiting lists. If we didn't have product, our collectors might go to other retailers. I also knew that we could sell everything that Cybis would give us, easily paying for the ad and then some. I accepted the offer and we ran our first full-page color ad in *Connoisseur* magazine.

Other dealers though I was crazy. They scoffed at me for what they saw as doing Cybis' advertising for them. However, I saw this as a way to get our name out on a national basis, at no true cost to us, since we would make up the expenditure in the sales of the additional figurines and reach an entirely new audience. What could be smarter?

At the time, I was looking for national visibility for the store, and this means of advertising was a perfect answer. We sold enough product to pay for the ad in a matter of weeks. I knew this would be the way for us to open up our national market even more and expose our fabulous products to this huge audience.

After watching some manufacturers use their entire advertising budget on three or four full-page ads, I began to experiment with smaller space advertising. I found that we didn't need to spring for a full-page ad all of the time. I found that we could stretch our budget to allow us to do that by using a half- or third-page ad as effectively, especially when the cost of the item didn't justify a full-page display. Most print advertising doesn't work well unless it's repeated several times. The smaller ads allowed us to achieve that all-important repetition in the same periodical that translated into successful customer recognition. Of course, we would take out a double-page ad, too, if the product warranted it. Analysis of the market and the art were the keys to success.

One of our great advertising success stories was with Waterford. The company had come out with a crystal heart pendant on a silver chain, priced at $35. I knew that this would be perfect for Valentine's Day. I also knew that other retailers would be banking on the pendant as a key item for their sales. So, with Waterford's approval, I took out an ad in the New Yorker three weeks before February 14. The manufacturer and others said the lead time was too far ahead—no one would purchase a Valentine's Day gift almost a month in advance. However, we sold more than 1,000 of them.

However, this created a slight problem. Waterford didn't have enough of the sterling silver chains for us to quickly fulfill our orders. Since fulfillment was something we took very seriously, they scrambled to find a new manufacturer who could get us the chains quickly. Our friend, Billy George, the president of Waterford USA, personally took it upon himself to locate a new supplier and have the pendants assembled and packed for us. As soon as they were finished, we picked them up and shipped the necklaces out with plenty of time to get there before Valentine's Day.

As I saw how well this program was working, I started to expand the magazines in which we appeared. Broadway's *Playbill* and the programs at the Garden State Arts Center hit the affluent, art aficionados that were some of our best repeat customers. For lower-priced items, we found that publications with greater reach, such as *The New Yorker*, *Smithsonian*, and *Gourmet* were great vehicles. We had successful ads in just about every major publication on the market, from *Town & Country* to *Architectural Digest*.

We developed quite an ability to match exactly the right product to the right magazine. By working effectively with the ad salespeople at the magazines—remember my theories on building relationships—we were able to get prime placement in the publications. In one case, I had found wonderful, and unique at the time, long-stemmed chocolate roses with beautiful green silk leaves—elegantly packaged as a dozen for $35—at a trade show. I immediately knew they would be a hit for Valentine's Day, so I placed an ad in *The New Yorker*, in the first quarter-page ad spot available, three weeks before the holiday. Again, I got negative feedback from other retailers. After all, who buys Valentine's presents weeks before Valentine's Day. Still, the ad worked. We sold more than 1,000 boxes of chocolate roses at $35 per dozen, packing them in ice and mailing them as far away as the Caribbean and Europe, and we were the first ones in the market to be associated with this popular product.

These ads were not only a driving force in bringing people into our store, but they added to the national demand for porcelain product. Soon, people from around the country and around the world were learning the Brielle Galleries name from the visibility that we had built through advertising. The signs were clear. As I chatted with one couple who came into our store, I learned they were from Staten Island. When I asked them how they happened to find Brielle Galleries, they mentioned that they had seen our ad in *The New Yorker* and if we could afford an ad in that publication, we must be good.

Ira's Business Rules

Stand Out from the Crowd

One thing about which I was never shy was letting people know about our store. From the very beginning, we tried to promote ourselves in ways that others never considered. Whether it was beach banners flown from airplanes or bartering product for advertising, my industry colleagues scoffed at us more than once. That mattered little to me—my main concern was whether the vehicle we were using would get our message out to the right audience. If it did, then we tried it.

Don't be afraid to take calculated chances in promoting your business. While you want to be sure that everything you do projects the right image, the only way that you'll rise above the advertising clutter is if you try to do things a bit differently than your competitors. Try new places to advertise, as long as they reach your target audience. Try new ways to showcase your product, using traditional or online tools. Whether you use events, demonstrations, infomercials, it's okay to experiment with new opportunities to help you expand your business. Don't be boxed in by what everyone else does. Being different is the only way that you can break out from the crowd.

Today, there are more opportunities than ever to use these multiple channels—in-store, online, direct selling, etc.—to open up your revenue streams and serve multiple markets. This allows you to grow your business while, at the same time, insulating it from the ups and downs of any one particular segment.

Our expanding profile also helped us become one of only eight locations in the country to sell Steuben glass. It took more than 17 years, but the venerable crystal company decided to test a group of pieces in two stores—ours and another store in the Midwest. We sold three $30,000 swan vases within days. Our sales so astonished the people at Steuben that they opened us as soon as possible, sending their own architects to help design the Steuben gallery at our location.

Since its launch in the '70s, our Porcelain Report had continued to grow in popularity. After several years, we changed the design to full-color and re-named it "A Quest for Excellence." It became a remarkable catalog of products ranging from our most affordable to our most exquisite.

While other catalogs would use their space to showcase 20 or 30 items, our limited budget required that we get the most bang for our buck. We would cram as many as 300 items into a single catalog, mixing high-end and lower-end piece, especially on the back page and on the order form, where impulse buys were likely to happen. I hired talented photographers and designers to make them look irresistible on the page. This was no small feat, as there was a great deal of competition for the customer's eye.

Eventually, the *Quest*, as we called it, grew to multiple pages and from a print run of 30,000 to a subscriber base of more than 500,000. *The New York Times* included it in a cover story about great catalogs, and it became one of our primary marketing vehicles. At one point, we ran a portion of it as an 8-page insert in the center of *Town & Country*. The next year, we left Town & Country and did a 12-page insert in *Architectural Digest*. The third year, opportunity knocked. We planned a 16-page insert in *Architectural Digest*. The magazine was planning to offset print it separately and made us an offer we couldn't refuse: If we ran the insert in November, they would give us December free. To the casual observer, this was a very expensive proposition. Of course, few knew that this was a matter of shrewd negotiation which netted us two months for the price of one. When new customers saw us running our insert in such an upscale publication for two months in a row, they were impressed. Such a big presence in one of the most exclusive consumer magazines made us famous.

On occasion, we would rent or trade lists to which we would send the catalog to increase sales. Retailers will sometimes make their mailing lists available for rent to other retailers in exchange for same. However, I was both surprised and pleased when we attempted to rent the list for the upscale retailer Gump's San Francisco and we were told that they would not rent it to us because they considered us too competitive. I couldn't understand why such an established retailer in a major city would be concerned about our store under a bridge on the Jersey Shore, in a town of only 3,400 people. That told me that other retailers were beginning to notice the ripples we were making in the pool of the national porcelain and luxury goods markets. We did convince them to exchange names, which ultimately benefited both stores.

In the end, we sold to a list of 70,000 of the top U.S. collectors of porcelain, crystal, silver and other fine goods. By the mid-80s, nearly 80 percent of our business was coming from outside of New Jersey, a result of the advertising, direct mail, and Ray's exceptional efforts developing relationships with individual collectors. Both Steuben and Tiffany approached us to rent our list, as they began to recognize the value of our customer base. At its peak, the Quest had grown to a circulation of more than 500,000 per year.

CHAPTER 12

Fruits of the Labor

The business was doing well, reaching $6 million per year. It had a list of wealthy and celebrity clients, a thriving catalog and corporate business, and a national advertising campaign. The sacrifices had paid off and the same studios and manufacturers to whom we had to prove ourselves were now approaching us to feature their products in our galleries and strategizing with us to figure out how to sell more and more product.

Our notoriety led to some interesting opportunities. For example, Nelson Rockefeller wanted to create replicas of his world-famous art collection in glass, wood, pewter and other materials. It was a way to bring this beautiful collection to a much broader audience by making a series of affordable pieces. We worked with the head of his foundation to launch the line, which we did at an event with an area hospital. Porcelain industry doyenne Mildred Mottahedeh, who created Rockefeller's own elaborate porcelain dinnerware service in Portugal, even made a personal appearance at the event.

One of the moments that made me see that we had really become a force in the industry was when the president of Baccarat, U.S.A. called me and asked me to come to his office. He wanted my opinion on a series of new products the company was creating for a major retailer. As I looked at the architectural drawings of a line of crystal inkwells, I knew we had to get the word out to our customers about these as soon as possible. I asked for a copy of the plans for the 23 crystal museum reproductions, as there were no samples available. He agreed, but thought it was a strange request.

We took those blueprints on the road and pre-sold $250,000 worth of 23 pieces with nothing but those architectural drawings. The company president was stunned that we were able to sell so many without having product, or even photographs. However, I knew that this was exactly the type of thing my customers would love. And I was right.

Being a part of Brielle Galleries during its heyday was an adventure. Our clients were so affluent and from such far-flung areas that, when we printed invitations to our shows and on our catalogs, we included directions via water and airplane. The people who owned those yachts in the marina—the ones I had considered a sign that our location might work out after all—were now our regular customers and friends. I dined in their homes, went to their children's weddings, and celebrated their lives with them.

One evening, I was just about to close the store and received a phone call from a woman who wanted to purchase an expensive three-section dish that had been featured in our catalog. I took the order, and there was something about her that seemed like she would be a perfect customer for Ray. I passed the order along to him for follow-up.

My instincts were correct. She was the daughter of a wealthy coal baron who made his fortune in the early 1900s and owned an estate in Europe. Her health was poor and she had a condition that required her to remain in a thermostatically controlled room most of the time. Her great joy was shopping and she owned a house adjacent to her primary residence where she kept all of her collections. Over the next several years, she purchased more than $2 million worth of items from us. Ray visited her frequently, sometimes with truckloads of items that he thought she would like. She usually bought all or most of them.

You never knew who would walk into the store, or what their needs would be. One thing that was a constant, however, was our commitment to service. Whether someone bought a vase or silver service, it was carefully unpacked, cleaned and repackaged. We even had special tea service cleaning flannels embroidered with the Brielle Galleries monogram. No detail was left unattended.

Sometimes, our commitment to service brought a few surprises. Ray had a customer in Pittsburgh who mentioned that he had purchased a Baccarat chandelier from another retailer. On his next visit to the customer, Ray examined the chandelier and found that it was a fake. The customer was irate that he had been cheated and vowed never to purchase items from anyone but Ray ever again.

He meant it. Not only did he buy all of his porcelain, crystal, silver and jewelry from us, he bought virtually every luxury item through Ray. One day, shortly before the December holidays, he called Ray and told him that his wife had purchased an expensive car for him. He wanted to buy her a beautiful fur coat in exchange. And he wanted to buy it from Ray.

Ray came to me, unsure of where to get a full-length sable coat, or if we could even help this customer. Of course, we didn't deal in fur, but I had a few contacts who were able to help us. The customer ended up buying four fur coats from us, through that connection—even flying in an Italian designer to ensure that the coats were fitted properly.

In the early 1990s, the Internet was also catching on full-force. This new tool made business operations more immediate, but it also opened up a world of options for customers. During this time, to remain competitive, manufacturers were also discounting their products through retailers and also offering them through their own factory stores and online, directly competing with retailers.

Ira's Business Rules

Breaking Rules

One day, a man drove into our parking lot in a shiny, expensive sports car. He came into the store and began looking at some of our porcelain sculptures. One of our employees showed him a pair of $250 Royal Copenhagen doves which he promptly dropped. They shattered into dozens of pieces.

I always believed that foolish rules were made to be broken. One of the rules of retailing that I never understood was the theory of "you break it, you buy it." Penalizing a customer for a clear accident never seemed to make much sense to me. After all, we were in the business of making customers feel good—not punishing them for accidents. While this customer apologized profusely and offered to pay for the doves, I wouldn't hear of it. Accidents happen. The customer ended up spending $3,000 in our store that day in return.

Actually, our policy was even more liberal than that. I always set aside money in our budget for losses sustained through breakage and returns. In one case, a customer had purchased a set of Waterford stemware. As always, we unpacked them from their boxes, examined them, cleaned them, and then carefully re-packaged them. The next day, she returned with them, broken. It was clear that this had happened after they left the store.

While my employees protested quietly, I refunded her money in full. I believed that keeping her happy was going to be far more beneficial to me in the long run than giving her a reason to criticize our good name to her influential friends.

I believe that liberal customer policies help you treat your customers as peers instead of putting up barriers between you. Successful retailing is a delicate balance of looking at the true cost of what may save you a few dollars in the short-run.

The first instances of retailer discounting were in sterling silver flatware. A major silver manufacturer agreed to allow a retailer in southern New Jersey to begin offering its products below suggested retail prices.

I argued with the manufacturer, explaining that these pieces were small, durable, and easy to ship—the retailer could undercut virtually any retailer in the United States in price. This was not the way to maintain the intrinsic value of these coveted products.

However, my arguments fell on deaf ears. At about the same time, the Federal Trade Commission determined that the fixed retail prices that many of our studios set were, in fact, restraint of trade, and made them illegal. Instead, the studios could only offer suggested retail prices, which retailers could then opt to discount. This opened the doors to deep discounters and mass market retailers, who could use their buying power to get better pricing from manufacturers, to offer sales on items that had previously not been offered for less than the studio's set value. This opened the flood gates for discounting on a level never seen before in this sector. Soon people were waiting for sales at Macy's or Fortunoff before they purchased their fine china and accessories.

Manufacturers were also discounting their products and competing directly with retailers. They were selling their products directly to the customer at prices that were below what we could profitably offer. This set up an adversarial relationship—we were competing with the very suppliers on whom we depended for unique, innovative products and marketing support. I fought all of this discounting like a tiger, but to no avail, as many manufacturers made their decisions based on the bottom line.

There was increasing competition from the Internet, where people could comparison shop virtually anywhere in the world. While this was impractical for items like large, complex porcelain sculptures or very heavy objets d'art, it was easy to price-hunt for easy-to-ship items. I also found evidence that manufacturers were mixing in current products with the discontinued merchandise at their outlet centers to unload items in which they were overstocked. However, the only discounting we did was in the form of special sales, which were held twice a year. Both were for very specific purposes, and more like events than simply discounting for the sake of discounting.

We decorated our store for the holidays in lavish fashion. After the holidays, we offered everything with a December holiday theme at 50 percent off. This did two things for us—it liquidated the inventory of holiday decorations so that we didn't have to store them. And it recouped the money we spent on the decorations, allowing us to re-invest in fresh, new decorations the following year. Only Christmas decorations and holiday-themed products were specially marked for the event, and we would usually sell out of holiday Lenox and Spode within an hour of allowing people through the door. There would be so many people lined up for the sale, often outside in the cold, that we would feed them coffee and donuts to keep them warm and in good spirits.

The only other sale that we had was called a "Countdown Sale." Customers could bid on the percentage of the retail price they would pay for an item through a closed bid from 20 percent to 50 percent off the retail price. Anyone who bid 10 percent could take the item home, but if they bid less, they had to wait until the sale was over to see whose bid was the lowest discount. The person who bid the lowest discount would be able to purchase the item, paying only that price. It became a good-natured competition for customers who wanted to get a bargain, but didn't want to lose out because they bid too low. It was a great exercise in psychology—some people would bid on items just because they saw a bid tag on them, indicating that others had bid on the item. So, they bid, too. They would call and ask us, "Did I win?" But there really wasn't anything to be won except being permitted to purchase a product at a discount.

Lisa and I would sit for hours every night for a week and do the math on the bids ourselves, figuring out the discounted prices. Lisa's math skills were strengthened through that exercise! Ultimately, she became a math tutor, which was the start of her business. To this day, she's like a human calculator.

Both of these events drove traffic into the store and resulted in other sales. But, more than anything, our success hinged on our exclusive product mix, personal sales, relationships and corporate business to maintain our profit margins, since I was unwilling to discount the way that the bigger department stores were. For the time being, this would work. However, the climate was changing and it was time to find new strategies for doing business.

CHAPTER 13

The Decision to Sell

Our company had long been attracting the attention of other retailers. Our corporate business had become a great success. Our catalog was reaching 500,000 people per year. And our retail business was stronger than ever. This also attracted the attention of investors who saw our catalog distribution, website, and global customer base as attractive assets, in addition to our famous beautiful galleries.

Discounting issue was beginning to become a problem for the industry. In 1995, an unexpected possibility came knocking when I was approached by a prominent businessman about acquiring the corporate business. I wasn't willing to part with a portion of the company. It made no sense to me to split the company up, as it worked best as a whole. Through his connections, however, we met a prominent publisher who became interested in the company. The publisher had long had a personal interest in creating luxury goods that were made in the United States, but had tried unsuccessfully to get a product line off the ground. He saw potential through Brielle Galleries to make this goal come to fruition.

At that time, the long-term future of Brielle Galleries was a question mark. Lisa and Daniel each had successful careers. While looking for work as an actress in New York, Lisa began tutoring students. She ultimately stopped acting to run her highly successful company, Inspirica, which by then had 100 employees. Dan became an attorney in Asbury Park, New Jersey and had been one of the youngest state assemblymen in New Jersey's history. Neither was interested in taking over the business, and I never found just the right person to groom for the role.

At the same time, I was nearing my 70th birthday. The work in the store included cleaning and carrying heavy boxes around. Moving product and fixtures around was exhausting work, but more than that, the draining tasks related to managing 40 regular employees and an additional 60 holiday staff members was beginning to take its toll, both physically and mentally.

Even so, at the time, I wasn't considering selling the company. However, the more I thought about the possibility of entrusting the company to a larger entity that could continue to grow it while allowing me to still service the customers who had been so loyal to us, definitely held appeal. The colleagues of the prospective buyer were internationally renowned professionals from the luxury gifts industry. They had resources that I would never be able to have, and the potential for growing the business was endless.

Lisa had loved the business and been involved with me in it all of her life. I was hesitant to broach the subject of selling it with her—I wasn't sure how she would react. I could have been selfish and tried to get her to take it over, but that wouldn't have been the right decision. Her business was going well, and she loved it. I didn't think that retailing was right for her—the long hours and the high overhead made it a constant challenge. The pressure of discounters was becoming more of a problem. At the time, she was living in New York City and would have had to moved to New Jersey. I also knew that she needed to continue on her own path, creating something new. We discussed the sale and she walked away with my blessing to run her own company.

As we talked, she turned to me and said, "Dad, we don't know what will happen. But whatever does happen, you need to be able to not look back with regret. You built this business. Now you have to let it go."

I considered whether I could do that. This business had been a huge part of my life for 45 years. But the opportunities for growth and longevity of the business seemed to lie with this unexpected proposition. I decided to sell the business.

The publisher gathered a group of investors to form a limited liability company that purchased the store. It included 22 of the finest professionals in luxury goods, publishing, technology and other sectors. A former executive from Steuben Glass would head up the company, and I would oversee the retail store operations without the distractions of the warehouse, administration, distribution and mail order businesses.

In late January 1996, just after the Christmas season, we signed the papers and I was no longer the owner of Brielle Galleries.

Ira's Business Rules

Creativity Has No Age Limits

You can create at any age—the process of making something happen in your life and in your business has no expiration date. That's one of the reasons why being an entrepreneur is so rewarding. No one can dictate to you what you can and cannot do when you own your own company.

Don't let your age or stage of life dictate what you can or can't do. The future holds limitless possibilities. Some of the projects I headed after the sale of the gallery were among the most exciting in my life.

CHAPTER 14

A Change in Focus

As part of the agreement with the store's buyers, I stayed on as president of Brielle Galleries. I would no longer be responsible for all operations of the business, including the catalog, warehouse, and corporate business. Instead, I would focus on the store and its operations. I also retained ownership of the buildings and property, as well as part of the inventory.

Of course, things were different with the new ownership. While Eleanor, Carolyn and Ray stayed on with the store, there were also new people brought in by the new ownership. Helene had left the company and went to work as a columnist for a local newspaper, a job that she loved.

The reorganization took a bit of adjustment, I welcomed the changes. The growth of the store into a multifaceted corporation had added layers between my customers and me. Meeting people and helping them discover the beauty and wonder of the objets d'art which we carried was what I loved about the business. Now, unencumbered by other responsibilities, I would be able to get back to the floor, working with the people who had been my friends and customers for so many years. I had always been the face of Brielle Galleries. Now, I would be free to focus on that aspect of the work and hand over the other areas to people who specialized in them.

What I soon learned was that running a corporation with investors is different than running a family-owned business. We had built our reputation on doing everything possible to make our customers happy, even if it cost us money in the short-term. Now, we had a new focus on analyzing each aspect of the business for its profitability.

This took time and took focus away from the no-holds-barred customer service for which Brielle Galleries had become known. If a customer called on a Saturday evening in need of a last-minute gift, I thought nothing of dropping it off on my way home. The new approach was to send the gift overnight by courier, such as FedEx or DHL, even if that meant it would arrive too late for the customer's needs. I spent most of my time on the floor with customers, but had little to say over policies and operations.

The changes that were taking place were exciting and intended to grow the business to new levels. Still, as I became more familiar with the new Brielle Galleries, I realized that this was no longer the business that I had built from a tiny, flat-roofed storefront in a bad location. It was a corporation with new priorities and a new focus. And I was an employee of the company, not the person calling the shots. After working with the company for less than two years, I decided that it was time for me to move on to new opportunities and new projects. I parted ways with the store in 1997.

Walking out the doors on that last day, knowing that I would no longer be part of running this store that I had built over nearly five decades, was difficult. I said my good-bye's to the staff, many of whom had become like my family. Inside, I mourned the little store that my mother and I had built so many years ago—the place where I was called to help for two weeks and where I spent nearly 50 years of my life. The Brielle Galleries that I knew was born with me and, in many ways, had died the day that I signed the closing papers on the sale.

At the time I left the store, I was 70 years old. Some people thought that I would retire and live a life of leisure. Obviously, those people didn't know me very well. I had a healthy inventory that I had retained from the sale, and also had my interest in Bronn. I saw a whole new world of opportunity. I immediately began to look for the next challenge, the next project. There were new business opportunities to be forged, and new charitable contributions to be made.

Three years after I left the business, in May of 1999, the new investors closed the doors of the store forever. The local newspaper, *The Asbury Park Press*, reported in June 1999, that the new owners had planned to phase out the retail end of the business and concentrate on the corporate

Ira's Business Rules

Letting Go

Once a business has been built into a profitable venture, it's likely that there will be someone, somewhere who is interested in buying it. That may be a competitor, or it may be someone who wants to own the type of business that you have created.

There are advantages to selling. Obviously, it's a way to recoup your investment of time, energy and resources in the business. It allows you to exit and move on to something else. However, it's not always an easy decision, and you need to be prepared for the fact that the business will undergo some significant changes. Sometimes, these are for the best; sometimes, they're not.

Letting go of something you've built from your own vision isn't easy. The key is to find a way to let go of the emotions tied to the business, including its future success or failure.

market but that the plan had floundered due to "a lack of needed financing," according to the company's chief executive officer. The report also said that the company's employee base was down to 20 in May of 1999.

I had been leasing the building back to them. In return for letting them break the lease, I negotiated the rights to my old mailing list of 75,000 individuals, as well as the records for hundreds of corporate accounts. While I didn't know what I would do with them at the time, recouping this information and the ability to contact these people, who had been my loyal customers for years, was something I felt was important, as the store closed. Little did I know what adventures lay ahead and how critical this information would become.

Ira's Business Rules

Family Businesses are Different than Large Corporations

The dynamics of a family-owned and run business are usually very different from those of large corporations. In organizations owned by investors and shareholders, the measurement of a business' success is often in dollars and cents only. And while it was always my goal to keep my business profitable, my measures of success went well beyond the bottom line. I cared about how my customers felt about our store. I looked for ways to create better service. I knew their names and had dinner at some of their homes. If a good customer had a last-minute need for something, I did everything in my power to deliver—even if it sometimes meant hand-delivering a piece on the way home from work or getting in my car and having something engraved immediately so that it would be picked up the next day for an important event.

When customers have come to depend on a certain type of service and that changes, it can be difficult for them to adjust. It's like an old friend who suddenly isn't there for you anymore. Consistency is key during any transition if you want to keep your customers happy and loyal.

CHAPTER 15

Rhapsody in Blue

In the two years after I left Brielle Galleries, I worked on selling the inventory that I had retained from the sale of the store, both online and through strategic placement in shops that sold it on consignment. It was stacked in my garage, which wasn't always convenient, but it kept me busy and allowed me to keep in touch with my customers, doing the work that I had loved for so many years. Still, I missed the shows that we had done at Brielle, not to mention the excitement of the galleries.

It was a spring day in 1998, when I received a call from longtime customer and friend, Betty Iselin, who was also the head and founder of the Monmouth Park Charity Fund. She informed me that I would be one of two honorees at the Monmouth Park annual Charity Ball, the foundation's premier fundraiser. This was a nonprofit that I had supported for many years through the store and the shows—I was deeply touched that they were taking the time to recognize me in this way.

Even more exciting was that my co-honoree was my longtime friend, restaurateur Joe Amiel. Joe's restaurant, The Old Mill Inn in Spring Lake Heights, was renowned for its fine food and celebrity clientele. He hosted shows at his restaurant with celebrities like Regis Philbin, Henny Youngman and Sammy Cahn. I had known Joe for years, and that made the announcement even more special for me.

Shortly after we became aware of the news, Joe called me to come to the restaurant for lunch. As we sat, enjoying the fine meal at his restaurant, Joe told me that he had some concerns about the foundation. The foundation had moved its galas away from the race track to be held in other locations. As a result, they weren't attracting the attendance that they used to attract when they were held at historic Monmouth Park, with its wonderful ambience; since the facility had been purchased by the state, it was no longer available to the group for their event. That was inhibiting the organization's ability to help the worthy area charities to which it dispersed millions and millions of dollars. This was of concern to both of us, since we had been so involved in the charity. We had both worked hard over the years to make sure that it was able to give money to the worthy organizations to which it distributed funds. To think that its largest fundraiser of the year was faltering was heartbreaking to both of us.

We both agreed that we could make a difference and, at that lunch, decided to take on an unprecedented level of involvement of the event's honorees to create an event to remember. After all, between my experience producing shows and his impeccable way with food and wine, we had exactly the combination of skills and contacts to make the event fantastic. I had recently learned that the 100th anniversary of the late George Gershwin's birthday was coming up. It was the perfect blend of entertainment and sophistication for this audience.

I called the chairwomen of the gala committee and arranged to meet with them. They loved the idea of George Gershwin's 100th—it was a great theme for a summer show. They voted immediately to give Joe and me the freedom to do it.

We had more than four hours to fill. The event started with a cocktail party and music. Then, we needed a wonderful dinner and time for dancing, along with a fundraising component, such as a silent auction. The evening usually ended with a drawing of some sort and the awards to the honorees.

Joe said that he would take care of supervising the food, and I had no doubt it would be wonderful. I began to scout the entertainment. One of the committee members was Gloria Monty, a producer for the television show "General Hospital." At one of the committee meetings, she pulled me aside.

"Ira, since you're doing this show, you've got to do something at the cocktail hour before the show, otherwise, you'll have people just standing around doing nothing," she said. I knew she was right. We had to start the evening off on the right foot.

I learned of a wonderful jazz pianist who was an expert on George Gershwin. He was perfect. I called Joe to tell him about this great pianist whom I thought we could get to play the cocktail hour. His name was Rio Clemente, also known as "The Bishop of Jazz."

Joe chuckled good-naturedly at my suggestion. Rio Clemente was far too great a musician to agree to play a charity ball cocktail hour, he said. There was no way he would agree.

Of course, that just made me more determined. I called Rio and asked him to participate, explaining the good work of the foundation. He agreed. Even better, as people entered the dining area, he would play "Rhapsody in Blue," accompanied by the dinner orchestra.

At the time, I admit that I didn't know much about Rio's background. It's a good thing I didn't know more about him when I asked him to play the Monmouth Park ball because I might have been intimidated. He had played in famous venues like Carnegie Hall and Lincoln Center. He was in demand at famous places like Manhattan's famed Birdland, the Oak Room at the Algonquin Hotel, and the West Bank Café's Laurie Beechman Theater.

It's a funny thing about people, though. If you ask most people to help a worthy cause, they will go out of their way to do it. It turned out that Rio was a native of Morristown, New Jersey and was aware of the foundation. Not only did he play our event—he did it for free and on his own portable piano, since we had no piano available for him to use during the cocktail hour—the grand piano was inside the dinner hall.

Next, I knew that we would need to make sure that people had fun and danced after dinner. In addition to a great orchestra, we needed dancers to get them excited to be up and on their feet. I called Newark's New Jersey Tap Ensemble. The director, Deborah Mitchell, had appeared in the movie, "The Cotton Club," and was the consummate professional. Eight of the dancers—four young men and four young women—would arrive in tuxedos and white tails, and impress the crowd with their dancing skills to the music of George Gershwin.

Ira's Business Rules

Shoot for the Stars

When you plan, plan big. And don't be afraid to ask for what you want.

People are surprisingly willing to help when you need it. By simply asking Rio Clemente to help our event, he agreed. You will often be pleasantly surprised by what you can accomplish by simply asking for what you need. The worst that can happen is that the individual in question will say "no." Then, you're no worse off than when you started.

This is true in business, too. People have found incredible mentors by just asking for their help. I believe that there is a willingness, within most people, to do what they can to help others. When you ask for the help you need, you may be shocked by the wonderful surprises that are in store for you.

The real draw, however, would be the guests of honor. Pierre Matisse, grandson of the famed Impressionist master Henri Matisse. Through my work with Very Special Arts and its director, Gene Maillard, I learned that Matisse had created a caricature poster depicting the musician playing the piano in honor of his 100th birthday. A portion of the poster's proceeds went to Very Special Arts, and Gene had approached me to see if I would carry the poster in my galleries. Through him, I contacted Pierre's representatives to see if he would attend. What happened was better than I ever expected. Not only would Pierre come, but George Gershwin's son, Alan, would be there, too, and play some of his music. It would be a truly authentic celebration of the master musician, with his only son in attendance, as well as the grandson of one of the most famous artists in history.

Carolyn and I worked on the publicity for the event using the media lists that had been developed from doing 41 shows at Brielle Galleries, as well as working in conjunction with the charity's PR person. Every time we had a celebrity at one of our events, we would hold a press conference that was attended by the state's most prominent media. We captured these names and used them to get the word out about Rhapsody in Blue, generating tremendous publicity, including interviews on local television stations and great print coverage. It was fantastic exposure for the charity.

As the word got out about the event, it started a buzz. Helene and I were out at a restaurant one night and a woman I didn't know approached our table.

"Ira, you don't know me, but I know your store. My husband hates to go to these charity things, but when we heard about this, he said he had to go. I can't get a ticket. Can you help me?"

Unfortunately, I couldn't. The attendance that had been dwindling was now a sell-out crowd of 500 people with 100 on a waiting list. That night was magical. People were dancing well past midnight, delighted at the wonderful music and food. It was just the spectacle needed to breathe new life into the gala.

113

I was honored to be a part of it and to be recognized in this way. But my true joy that night came from continuing the legacy of such a worthy organization that helped so many nonprofits in the area. Now that I didn't have the day-to-day responsibilities of the store, I could go out and spend time creating exciting events like this. And there were plenty more to come.

CHAPTER 16

Luxury Galleries

It was 2001 when I got a call from my daughter, Lisa, inviting me to go to a seminar with her. It was a meeting of the Luxury Marketing Council of New York City, where representatives from some of the top luxury goods manufacturers share ideas and invite guests to share information that can benefit their businesses. Lisa was a member of the group, as her company is a high-end provider of tutoring and educational services.

This particular seminar featured a famous patent attorney who specialized in Internet law, which was a new concept at the time. As I listened to the speaker discuss this lightning-fast medium for reaching a worldwide audience, an idea started to form in my mind. While discounting had changed the way that many luxury goods retailers had to do business, this was an opportunity to reach people who had no other way of accessing these pieces of art and eliminate this problem.

When Brielle Galleries had closed, I had the rights to my mailing list and corporate clients revert back to me as part of the deal for letting the new owners break their lease. I also had about 100 pieces of inventory that I had retained. I had a following and this new tool to reach an entirely new audience. I was back in business.

Since the investors still owned the rights to the Brielle Galleries name, I needed to come up with a new one. I thought about it and it seemed best to keep it simple, yet reminiscent of the business that I had built before. I decided on the name: Luxury Galleries.

The next challenge was a space to house the merchandise. It made sense to have a showroom that could serve as a retail location as well, since my local customers were used to having a location to visit. It also made sense that our location could produce retail revenue. On August 22, 2002, we opened the doors to Luxury Galleries, a 5,000 square foot showroom in the Brielle Galleries building. It was a location that I owned and which customers were used to. I was home again.

Even though we had this location, I wanted the focus of the business to be on Internet sales. It was a new frontier—I was entering an e-commerce world that I knew little about, competing against people who were half my age. But I had never backed down from a challenge before. I certainly wasn't going to start now.

It was important to me that the website adhered to the same standards of excellence that the galleries had. The site would have virtual galleries, just as we had brand-specific galleries. I wanted people to be delighted by what they saw online, just as they had been overwhelmed by what they had seen in our galleries. That required the same beautiful photography and perfection in design that we had used in our catalog and other promotional materials. In addition, I would bring a personal touch to the Internet. We would recreate the business that we had built in Brielle in an online setting.

I knew that I couldn't do this without Carolyn. She had been so important to my business and managed our corporate clients with such finesse. I knew that this medium would be a perfect place to apply her skills. She and a handful of my former employees helped us get the business off of the ground. I hired a talented web designer who understood my vision for the site.

I still had more than $100,000 worth of merchandise remaining after the sale of the galleries. We created beautiful displays and successfully attracted back a strong population of our former clients. What was most exciting was watching the website take off. We were able to create a great

Ira's Business Rules

Embrace New Ways of Doing Things

Of course, by today's standards, our LuxuryGalleries.com website was a bit rudimentary. We didn't have animation, video, podcasts or many of the other interactive features that websites have today. However, our site, with its striking black and gold motif, was beautifully designed for the time in which it operated. It allowed us to recreate a successful business in a record amount of time. We were able to get up and running in a few months and begin generating revenue. It really was true that the Internet turned our business hours into 24 per day.

But if I hadn't been open to completely re-vamping the way we did business, I would have missed out on this important opportunity. It would have been easy to dismiss the Internet—as many did at the time—as a trend that wouldn't last. We all know how wrong that prediction was!

Technology keeps evolving at the speed of light. As you progress through your entrepreneurial career, don't become so set in your ways that you lose sight of the importance of innovation. There's always a new or better way of doing something. The more you integrate change and efficiency into your business while embracing opportunity, the more longevity and success you will have.

mix of extremely high-end artwork, as well as lower-end pieces. There was something for everyone. We focused on getting our site ranked well with search engines and doing some e-mail blasts to our customer base. Soon, sales from the website were increasing to a rate that let us purchase more inventory to sell through the site.

One of the great things about the Internet was also the ability to include information about the artists and the artwork. This tied into my theory that it was critical to educate customers about the pieces they were buying. We included background information about the various studios and artist bios of everyone from pewter and enamel sculptor Brian Rodden to painter Edna Hibel to Disney illustrator and artist Carl Barks.

The website also gave us a fantastic, interactive home for the corporate gifts division. Instead of Carolyn carrying a small selection of options to them or being limited by the number of items we could fit in a catalog, we now had endless space to showcase our offerings. This was very convenient for our corporate customers who enjoyed the option to shop for their company needs any time of the day or night.

CHAPTER 17

The White House Anniversary

I had been running Bronn of America since the mid-1970s. I was looking for new opportunities for us to achieve a higher profile for the studio, which was now being managed by porcelain artist Stephen Weston, a gifted modeler and painter.

It was just before the turn of the century when Gene Maillard called me. He was on the national council of the White House 200th Anniversary committee and educational outreach program for American children. The funds raised from the event would help educate approximately 3 million children in grades 5 through 8. While I explained to him that I no longer had Brielle Galleries, I also knew that this was a wonderful opportunity to help children—something that has always been a priority for me. So, I told him I would do what I could to help.

Of course, the solution would be to produce an event—something at which we excelled. But we would need something wonderful to attract people. I had always loved the handmade St. Petersburg Collection of porcelain eggs made by Theo Fabergé. They were different from the more famous Fabergé eggs made in France, but they were exquisite, and we had carried many of them at Brielle Galleries. One of the features, besides their beauty, that made them so beloved, was that each egg housed a small treasure inside. It would be perfect to create an egg that held a surprise of a miniature White House.

There was one challenge, however. In order for such a piece to be accepted into the White House as a gift, it had to be made in America. Fabergé was based in England. Although the company, and especially its leader, Theo Fabergé, who was the only surviving grandson of the legendary Carl Fabergé, had tried to create pieces for the White House in the past, it had never worked out because his studio did not have operations in the U.S.

Stephen and I realized that forming a strategic alliance with Bronn might be exactly the opportunity that we were looking for. By working with Theo, who would design the egg, we could then produce it here in the U.S.—an authentic Theo Fabergé egg produced in the Bronn Studio. When we approached Theo's company, they loved the idea and enthusiastically agreed to work with us.

Carolyn immediately set to work gathering research. We conducted site inspections at the Quincy, MA home of John and Abigail Adams, the first President and First Lady to live in the White House. We visited 1600 Pennsylvania Avenue ourselves and took note of the décor and appointments, as they would be integral to the design of the egg. In the end, Carolyn had a mountain of research, photographs, sketches and notes which were shared with Theo's team.

They went to work designing the egg. It was magnificent and no detail was left to chance. Elements from early White House exterior décor were incorporated into the egg. Hand-painted portraits of John and Abigail Adams adorned each side. Inside was a beautiful gold replica of the original White House.

However, I had more ideas up my sleeve. We had a long and successful relationship with Waterford. I approached them about creating a special commemorative bowl, mounted on a beautiful wood base. The pieces would be designed by the crystal artisans in Ireland. Waterford created a magnificent bowl with oval-shaped, elongated cuts that recreated the panes of one of the Palladian windows in the White House. Cuts that interpreted the garlands embellishing the White House made the bowl a uniquely American piece.

And, of course, I had to involve my dear friend and longtime colleague Edna Hibel. She has been called "America's best-loved artist" by many, and her pieces are known for their hope, beauty and compassion. She created fine art giclées, a form of reproduction that looked like photographic copies, of her painting, *The Heart and Conscience of America*, as a tribute to the White House 200th anniversary and to the children of the world. The painting featured the White House in the background, with more than 20 children in the foreground.

When Carolyn and I reviewed the plans for these incredible pieces, we couldn't believe what was taking shape. This was going to be big. And we needed a big party to go with it.

In the meantime, I called Congressman Frank Pallone, a Democrat from New Jersey and someone who had been a longtime friend, to ask for his help with the event in Washington, D.C. He sponsored us, and we contacted The Congressional Club, who would host the unveiling of the egg at the First Lady's Reception and Luncheon in May. We discovered that, on the day we wanted to host the event, there would be six parties all over Washington. So, Congressman Pallone reserved a smaller room that would hold 200 people. After all, with so many parties, he thought we shouldn't expect a large turnout.

We invited a number of our customers, as well as Washington V.I.P.s and celebrities that Gene knew. We estimated that we might have 50 or so people at the event. We had been loaned a list of the who's-who of Washington elite after meeting with some of the leaders of the Congressional Club and showing them the three pieces. We knew it was a long shot to invite all of these high-ranking figures in the political system, but we also knew that it wouldn't hurt to let them know about the event. The hold-the-date notice of the group ended up having a half-page announcement about our event, right next to a piece about a program being held by Cokie Roberts.

We were wrong about the attendance. As the responses started to pour in, the guest list reached over 200—too big for the room that Congressman Pallone had reserved for us. Fortunately, we had a former employee who was employed within the Republican party. Through her connections, we reserved a second room, with capacity for about 350 people. However, our response list outgrew that room, too. We finally landed a room in the Dirksen wing of the Senate, thanks to her gracious assistance and the help of Senator Trent Lott, ending up with an attendance of nearly 400 people, including 110 congressmen, 10 U.S. senators and other luminaries.

The day of the event was wonderful. The Theater Chamber Players, a professional music ensemble dedicated to presenting contemporary chamber music to the people of metropolitan Washington, D.C., provided the entertainment. The Chamber Players were a great choice because of their commitment to exposing children to chamber music through an active outreach program.

Stephen demonstrated how the egg was made, and the audience was mesmerized. Edna Hibel was on hand to meet and greet the people in attendance. PBS came and filmed her at the event. While we were not allowed to sell anything there, we did liquidate the equivalent of all of the inventory that we had of the three amazing products—the porcelain eggs, the crystal bowls and the giclée reproductions of Edna's magnificent painting—by taking the names and contact information of people at the event who were interested in the pieces. We followed up with them and took their orders.

Most of all, the Theo Fabergé egg put the Bronn Studio on the map. From an appearance on the Washington, D.C. area's NBC morning show to national newspaper coverage to an event that included some of the most powerful people in Washington, the event was such a success that, the next year, I received a call from a Republican member of the Congressional

Club, asking if we would come back and host an event for Laura Bush. I was interested, and went to the Lenox showroom to discuss it with them.

I told them that I would like to strip their showroom of every Presidential dinnerware service since Abraham Lincoln's. The were thrilled at the idea. However, we were ultimately unable to do that event, since we didn't have appropriate product to liquidate in order to make it pay off. Still, it was an honor to be asked and proved that opportunities were still presenting themselves years after selling Brielle Galleries.

Ira's Business Rules

Enlist Help

By reaching out to the artisans who created the wonderful pieces for this event, we were able to create a memorable and festive occasion filled with beautiful things. The Theo Fabergé egg and Waterford bowl and the Edna Hibel giclée received marvelous publicity nationwide. In addition, by asking for help from Congressman Pallone and members of the Democratic and Republican parties, we were able to change the accommodation for our event, which was many times what we originally expected it to be.

Use your network and ask for help when you need it. Sometimes, you need to do things on your own. Other times, you need to rely on others to take what you can do to the next level. Don't be afraid to ask.

CHAPTER 18

Remembering One of Our Own

There were so many people in the New York and New Jersey area who were directly affected by the terrorist attacks of 9/11/01. In the days after the shocking events, I learned that Paul Keating, the son of Muriel Keating, one of my longtime employees and friends, had been killed when the buildings fell.

I had not known her son, who was only 38 years old when he died, but by all accounts, he was an outgoing and fun child. He was in his 30s when he was living in downtown Manahattan and had decided to become a New York City firefighter. On the day of the attacks, he had been on the phone with one of his sisters when he heard about a plane hitting the first tower. Although he was off duty, he told her that he was going to go downtown to see if he could help. That was the last time that anyone ever spoke to Paul, whom his parents and five brothers and sisters called "Paulie."

The effects of that day were felt around the world. In the Waterford studio in Ireland, the artisans were so devastated by the attacks that they felt they needed to express their grief through their artistry. The wife of one of the crystal artists had seen a photograph of firefighters raising an

American flag at Ground Zero. She suggested that it would make a perfect crystal piece.

Two of the artisans set about creating an engraving of that photo on a piece of crystal shaped like a New York City firefighter's hat. The piece was stunning, and Waterford sent it to one of the largest, New York City department stores, as they thought that someone in the United States would want to purchase it as a remembrance. As a gesture of good faith, its $10,000 price would be donated to a charity that benefited deceased firefighters and their surviving spouses and children. There it sat, surprisingly, without any interest from collectors.

Eventually, Waterford sent the piece to me for display at Luxury Galleries. Muriel immediately fell in love with the piece, which reminded her so much of her son. Having the piece in the store gave her comfort, and it was clear that she really wanted it for her own. Still, its price tag was hefty, even though the money would go to a good cause.

Shortly after the piece arrived, I got a phone call from Muriel's husband, Neil. He told me that he planned to purchase the sculpture and that he would have the money to me within a few days. He asked me not to sell the sculpture to anyone else, and I agreed.

The next day, I got a call from a heartbroken widow from western Monmouth County whose husband had been a battalion fire commander and had died in the attacks. She had heard about the sculpture, and she insisted on purchasing it. I had to explain to her that I could not sell the piece. The next day, she showed up at the gallery with a $10,000 check anyway, weeping and pleading with me to buy the sculpture. Turning her away was one of the hardest things that I have ever done.

Later that week, on Muriel's day off, Neil arrived to purchase the sculpture. We packaged it carefully and he took it out of the store to hide at his daughter's house. The next day, when Muriel arrived at work, she was heartbroken to see the sculpture missing.

"Where is it?" she asked.

"Oh, we had a collector come in and buy it," I replied, afraid she would press me for details.

"Well, they really should have left it here until Christmas so that people could see it," she said sadly.

That was the last time that she mentioned the statue.

On Christmas Eve, Muriel's birthday, her family gathered at her daughter's home. After dinner, Neil disappeared down into the basement. No one in the family, not even their daughter who was hosting the party, knew what he had done. He carefully brought the package upstairs and put it on the table before Muriel. She opened the sculpture, shocked at what she saw. That night, there were tears of happiness at the wonderful surprise that Neil had arranged and tears of sadness as everyone remembered their devastating loss. That is the kind of power that art can have.

When I found out that Muriel and Neil had arranged a trip to Ireland the following spring, I called my contacts at Waterford and arranged for a V.I.P. tour for them. They visited the factory and were able to try their hands at cutting crystal. They met with the president of the company and the artisans who had created the 9/11 sculpture. They had a deep connection to the artisans through the one-of-a-kind sculpture.

The money was ultimately donated to the New York Police and Fire Widows' and Children's Benefit Fund, a charity that was launched by famed baseball legend Rusty Staub. Because the transaction had taken place through Luxury Galleries, we were invited to present the $10,000 check at a benefit at Gracie Mansion, where Mayor Michael R. Bloomberg hosted a reception. As I learned more about the event, I found that two executives from financial firms would be honored for donating millions at the same event. I was a bit intimidated and told Carolyn that I was hesitant to give our $10,000 check—which we had blown up to 6-feet long for a bit of dramatic impact—when they were giving so much money. She insisted that I go and deliver the check when Mayor Bloomberg asked for it during the large press conference.

Ira's Business Rules

Do Good

Your business, in addition to being something that provides you with work and a livelihood, can also be used to make a difference. Of course, there was no personal profit for me in handling the 9/11 sculpture. And I had no idea how important this would become to someone dear to me. The sculpture, to this day, sits in a place of honor in the Keatings' home—a remembrance of their beloved son, Paul, who died a hero, trying to help other people. It was, once again, my business and the contacts I had made through it that brought me this opportunity to be a part of something so important.

Look for ways to make your business an instrument that makes the world a better place. It might be getting involved in charities, or using environmentally conscious business practices, supporting education or finding other ways to give back to your community. Of course, this has some business benefits, but that's not the reason why you should do it. There has to be more to your work than just profit. Finding ways to make a difference can add a whole new dimension to what you do every day and give you renewed enthusiasm for the hard work that it often takes to be an entrepreneur. After all, there is no feeling like knowing that you've truly made a positive difference in someone's life. As business owners, we have the obligation and the privilege to use our enterprises to do just that.

We walked into Gracie Mansion and were overwhelmed by the luxury. While Mayor Bloomberg had opted not to live in the traditional mayor's residence, choosing to remain in his own home, the Mansion was a lovely place to host events such as this. Deep Wedgwood blue walls with white trim made the room look rich and elegant. Throughout the event, no detail was overlooked. This was my kind of place.

The people in attendance, which included the entire Keating family, the Mayor and Rusty Staub, himself, were as enthusiastic as if we were giving millions. Mayor Bloomberg was incredibly gracious and kind, paying personalized attention to us, even though there were approximately 200 guests. Neil and Muriel had brought the crystal statue, which was placed on the mantle behind the podium, visible to all in attendance. At the event, they did a beautiful tribute honoring Paul Keating. It was a day that I'll never forget—and a day that brought a bit of light into the Keatings' devastating loss.

CHAPTER 19

New Opportunities

Throughout the years, Bronn of America's reputation for quality continued to present new opportunities for projects. Part of the reason for this was the relationships I had built through Brielle Galleries and Luxury Galleries. I had a number of colleagues who were interested in the high-quality, American-made porcelain that we produced.

One of those colleagues, Bruce Hamilton, owned a successful comic book and high-end memorabilia store in Arizona, and published a catalog of Disney-related products. He was acquainted with Ray and knew about Bronn's excellent work. In 1997, Bruce contacted us, through Ray, about getting involved in a new project.

At the time, he was a licensee of the late Carl Barks' artwork. Barks was a famed Walt Disney illustrator who passed away in 2000. He was most famous for creating Duckburg, a fictional city that appears in Walt Disney comic books. Barks was the talent behind many of Duckburg's most famous residents including Scrooge McDuck and Gladstone Gander, among others. His talent for working on ducks earned him the nickname "The Duck Man."

Ray wanted to produce porcelain sculptures of a selection of 10 of Barks' many, many paintings, with Bruce's support. He knew that we had the ability to produce porcelain of a quality that would easily meet the Disney company's approval. The pieces would be sold through Bruce's gallery and catalog. When Carl saw the prototype that we created in conjunction with Connoisseur, he enthusiastically endorsed the idea.

Bruce was wise about marketing porcelain sculptures. For the pieces we produced, he quickly established a secondary market by selling the piece numbered 1 at $13,950. Owning the first piece in a collection is always valued. He then priced the pieces numbered 2 through 10 at $8,950. Then, he sold the remaining pieces at approximately $6,950. They sold out almost immediately.

The contacts kept coming. When Sir Andrew Lloyd Webber was looking for someone to create his porcelain sculptures for Phantom of the Opera, he reached out to Connoisseur, asking them who could create porcelain sculptures of "Cats" and "Phantom of the Opera." He sent us artwork from the production, and we discussed licensing the products. When Webber saw the quality of our work and some of our initial plans for the porcelain sculptures, he was enthralled. He would be issuing licenses to his characters and designs through his company, the Really Useful Group. However, he wanted input in the creation of the characters and where they would be sold. Since it was important for me to protect customers from price differentials in different markets—and the proposed arrangement would allow undercutting prices via currency exchanges and dealers—we decided that the arrangement wasn't a good fit. We wished each other well and moved on.

Bruce proved to be a valuable contact once again, making a connection to what was probably the grandest project that we ever undertook. In 1993, Bruce approached Ray to work with him on the porcelain sculptures for a new theme park based on L. Frank Baum's beloved classic,

The Wizard of Oz. In 1992, the L. Frank Baum Trust gave its approval for Robert Kory's Oz Resorts and Entertainment, Inc. to support development of "The Wonderful World of Oz" theme park in Kansas City, Kansas. The company would use images and characters from the 1939 MGM film musical starring Judy Garland, Bert Lahr, Jack Haley, and Ray Bolger.

The result would be a 900-acre theme park outside of Kansas City. Kory and Oz wanted us to handle the porcelain sculptures, which was very exciting. Bronn would be producing some of the best-known characters in children's literature and cinema. In addition, we would be crafting a massive bronze sculpture of Dorothy, Toto, Scarecrow, the Tin Man, and Lion that would welcome visitors to the park, as long as we got a corporate sponsor and Kory approved it.

We went to work creating a miniature model of the entrance sculpture and sent it to the Oz offices. They were thrilled. The features were lifelike and true to the original actors, including Judy Garland, Jack Haley, Ray Bolger, and Bert Lahr. All we needed was a corporate sponsor to underwrite the full-scale work.

At the same time, we created a prototype of a Scarecrow porcelain sculpture from the movie. Carolyn was heading to a wedding in California and brought it with her to deliver to the Oz headquarters, which was near where she was going to be. A representative from the office called, thrilled with the quality and artistry of the piece. We felt we had a good chance to land the contract to produce the line.

Oz secured the $500 million in funding and the approvals that it would need to get the park off the ground. However, we learned later that, for some reason, the park plans were being shelved. Apparently, local residents fought the park successfully, and it would not open as planned. We were disappointed that we wouldn't be able to work with Kory, who was an incredible visionary and would have made the park a spectacular destination.

Bronn ran successfully until the early 1990s, when Stephen and I decided that it was time for me to retire and for him to pursue other opportunities. I wasn't interested in taking on more major projects at 75. I had sold the website and corporate division, which limited the ways I could liquidate product and I wanted to sell the building. It was time to move on to a new phase in my life. Stephen continues to be one of the best porcelain restorers in the United States and works out of his gallery, Weston Galleries, in Manasquan, New Jersey.

Of course, the Bronn of America studio had specialized kilns that were very expensive. I wanted to donate them to an art school that could use them. I tried to donate them to Rutgers University and to Monmouth

Ira's Business Rules

Go for It

We were involved in a series of amazing opportunities with some of the finest companies and creative people in the world. When opportunity presented itself, I would first evaluate it, and most of the time I would get involved. Many of these involvements held some kind of risk, especially the risk of losing the investment of whatever time we put into the endeavor. But, more often than not, they paid off in the long run. Even when they didn't pay off in money, they paid off in great experiences and contacts.

It's easy to stay safe and not take risks. However, few people get to live their lives to the fullest by taking the easy route. Seek out exciting experiences and take on challenges full speed. It is the best way to grow.

University, but they were too big to fit into their studios! Finally, a friend suggested donating them to New Jersey's Grounds for Sculpture, a renowned 35-acre sculpture park and museum in Hamilton. The studios there had only worked with bronze in the past. These kilns would expand their capabilities to experiment with porcelain. It was good to know that these tools were going to continue their good work, providing educational opportunities for students and creating beautiful works of art for everyone to enjoy.

Epilogue

When I think back on the twists and turns that my life has taken, I realize that I wouldn't trade any of them. Being an entrepreneur is something that gets in your blood. It's the ability to call the shots in your own business and make your vision a reality. While companies today have gotten smarter about allowing employees to act more like entrepreneurs—taking more ownership of their ideas and acting more quickly without a lot of corporate red tape involved—there's still nothing like the thrill of watching a business that you have patiently grown now succeed.

Of course, it's not always easy. Many times you may feel as though you're walking a tightrope without a net underneath you. This can cause sleepless nights, especially when you have the responsibilities of a family, a home and the livelihoods of employees. However, being your own "boss," so to speak, actually gives you more control over your destiny and your earning potential than working for someone else does. When you lose a job, it may come without warning and may take you months or even years to recover. When you own your own business, monitoring its growth, cash flow and profits, you have a much better sense of its ability to support you.

You can make changes to improve your situation, or you can change your course entirely.

Throughout this book, I've shared with you the most important lessons that I have learned as someone who has been a life-long entrepreneur. I overcame many odds and proved many naysayers wrong. If I had to pick two key factors to my success, I would say that they are honesty and persistence.

Why are these most important? Well, first and foremost, being honest and having integrity in your business gives you a solid reputation and name. That's something that no amount of marketing can do for you—it has to come from how you run your business. Having a reputation for honesty builds relationships. When you do the right thing in your business, you develop customers who are not only loyal, but who want you to succeed. They help you in ways that you never imagined—by referring new customers, by helping you find resources and contacts you need to grow your business, by providing suggestions and feedback that make a difference.

Persistence is important because no measure of success comes without effort. Every business is going to face obstacles and setbacks. It is in the face of those obstacles that you develop strength. You need to dig in and find ways to overcome the challenges that you will face. When you triumph over a challenge—no matter how big or small—your business grows stronger, as does your belief in yourself and what you can accomplish. If you give up at the first sign of a struggle, you won't be in business for very long.

Of course, there are many other qualities and resources that you'll need to run your business effectively. You need to have a vision and creativity. You need to have the ability to put your ego aside and do what's best for your business. You have to keep on top of new developments in your industry and be flexible—no business can do things exactly the same way year after year because markets and opportunities evolve.

I owe a lifetime of memories and experiences to that shop under the bridge in Brielle. I am very grateful to it. While Brielle Galleries required an incredible commitment from me over the years, it also provided me with many things. It supported my family for decades, and it provided me with lifelong friendships with customers, employees, and vendors. It was the realization of my vision. Every time I cashed my paycheck, I knew that this was something that I had not only earned, but created from scratch.

For all who are reading this book, I offer my best wishes and encouragement. I hope that you have enjoyed this walk through the life of one entrepreneur and one spectacular business. It is my sincere hope that you enjoy the success of your dreams.

Ira Jacobson